PACE Yourself

A Handbook for ESL Tutors

Teresa S. Dalle and Laurel J. Young

TESOL **Teachers of English to Speakers of Other Languages, Inc.**

Typeset in Cochin and Serif Gothic Display
by Capitol Communications Systems, Inc., Crofton, Maryland USA
Printed by Kirby Lithographic Company, Arlington, Virginia USA
Indexed by Coughlin Indexing Services, Annapolis, Maryland USA

Teachers of English to Speakers of Other Languages, Inc.
700 South Washington Street, Suite 200
Alexandria, Virginia 22314 USA
Tel. 703-836-0774 • Fax 703-836-6447 • E-mail info@tesol.org • http://www.tesol.org/

Director of Communications and Marketing: Helen Kornblum
Managing Editor: Marilyn Kupetz
Copy Editor: Ellen Garshick
Cover Design: Capitol Communications Systems, Inc.

The Case Studies are composites of real tutoring events with many different students. All names of tutors and students are pseudonyms.

Figure 2 (Sample Cloze Passage) and Passages for Assessing Reading Skill in chapter 4 adapted from *Essays and Arguments, Section Two*, by I. Johnston, 2000, http://www.mala.bc.ca/~johnstoi/arguments/argument2.htm. Copyright released May 2000.

Site sample in chapter 8, Figure 1, from *Adult Education Teachers Guide*, by C. R. Graham and M. M. Walsh, 1996, http://humanities.byu.edu/elc/teacher/teacherguidemain.html. Reprinted with permission.

Site sample in chapter 8, Figure 2, from *The Seasons*, by N. Coghlan, 2002, ESL Lounge, http://www.esl-lounge.com/level2/lev2seasons.html. Copyright 2001–2002 by Neil Coghlan. Reprinted with permission.

Site sample in chapter 8, Figure 3, from *Basic Composition Assignment on Adjectives*, by Pearson Adult Learning Centre/The Educated Web, 2002, New Westminster, British Columbia, Canada: New Westminster School District 40, http://palc.sd40.bc.ca/palc/bcassign/bcfeb4.htm. Copyright 2002 by Pearson Adult Learning Centre. Reprinted with permission.

Site sample in chapter 8, Figure 4, from *Main Characters*, by S. Kemley, 2000, http://www.eslcafe.com/pv/pv-b.html. Copyright 2001 by abcteach.com. Reprinted with permission.

Site sample in chapter 8, Figure 5, from "Dennis Oliver's Phrasal Verbs: B," by D. Sperling, 2002, *Dave's ESL Café*, http://www.eslcafe.com/pv/pv-b.html. Copyright 2002 by Dave's ESL Café. Reprinted with permission.

Site sample in chapter 8, Figure 6, from "Amazing Animals," by J. Haynes, 1999, *everythingESL*, http://www.everythingesl.net/lessons/animalstwo.php. Copyright 2000 by J. Haynes. Reprinted with permission.

Site sample in chapter 8, Figure 7, from *How to Pronounce -ed in English*, by J. Essberger, n.d., Cambridge, England: English Club, http://pronunciation.englishclub.com/-ed.htm. Copyright 2002 by englishclub.com. Reprinted with permission.

ISBN 1-931185-06-9

Library of Congress Control No. 2002114955

Contents

Unit 1: Prepare

Unit 2: Assess

Unit 3: Construct

Unit 4: Evaluate

Preface

Thank you for choosing *PACE Yourself: A Handbook for ESL Tutors,* a guide for inexperienced or volunteer tutors of ESL who may or may not have training in ESL teaching methodology. We do not claim that this text will make overnight experts of novices. Instead, our aim is to provide an easy-to-follow guide that gives a starting point and resources to people who want to tutor one to four nonnative speakers of English at a time but do not know how to go about it.

Most of the information in this handbook is geared toward tutors who are working with ESL students ranging from the beginning to the intermediate level, as, in our experience, most advanced-level students seek professional tutors or teachers when they need outside help. However, we describe (in chapter 4) the skills that identify all levels, including advanced, and we suggest activities and materials (in Appendix A) that are appropriate for all levels.

How Is the Book Organized?

PACE is an acronym for four steps in the tutoring process (*p*repare, *a*ssess, *c*onstruct, and *e*valuate), which correspond to the four units of the text. We begin with three case studies, composites of actual tutoring situations, that illustrate three different but equally common tutoring scenarios: a small group of refugees, an elementary school student, and a professional adult. Following the case studies, each unit contains three chapters that describe an important step in the tutoring process. The chapter titles are based on questions frequently asked by practicum students and volunteer tutors. At the end of each chapter, we show how the tutors in the case studies applied the step described in that chapter to their tutoring situations. For your convenience, most chapters also include reproducible forms. The Guide to Topics provides an easy means of locating specific information in the text.

The four appendixes contain further information for ESL tutors. Appendix A includes annotated lists of ESL texts of various types for various language levels and numerous Web sites offering lesson plans, exercises, games, visual aids, and other materials. Appendix B defines commonly used ESL terms that tutors are likely to encounter when checking other sources of information about teaching ESL. Appendix C lists contact information for some of the best known publishers of ESL texts and materials. Appendix D lists professional organizations that are helpful to ESL tutors.

How Should I Use This Book?

We recommend that you examine the three case studies before studying other parts of the text to gain a better understanding of what ESL students of different ages and educational backgrounds need, how tutors go about meeting those varied needs, and what you need to know before you begin tutoring.

Some parts of the text may at first seem irrelevant to your immediate tutoring needs. However, we ask that you examine them anyway because they all contain basic guidelines that successful teachers of ESL follow. If you are both untrained and inexperienced in the field of ESL, we especially recommend that you read chapter 6, which discusses personal, cultural, and linguistic factors that can affect the student's learning style and behavior. Note that we have intentionally repeated important concepts throughout the book to make sure you have the information you need no matter which age group or language skill you focus on in your tutoring.

We hope that this handbook meets your needs as a beginning tutor of ESL and that it will be your key to many hours of rewarding and successful tutoring.

Acknowledgments

We thank Kathleen Graves, Marilyn Kupetz, and Ellen Garshick, of TESOL, who patiently examined and advised us on improvements for this book; Teresa Dalle's husband, Reginald, and children, Eric and Emilie, for their encouragement; and Laurel Young's husband, Dick; her sons, David and Stephen; and her mother, Betty Archer, for their support. Finally, we thank all the colleagues, friends, teachers, and tutors who have provided valuable input and encouragement throughout this project.

Guide to Topics

Topic	Chapter											
	1 Gather information.	2 Acquire frequently used tutoring tools.	3 Follow an organized format.	4 Assess skills and determine students' goals.	5 Use assessment to determine tutoring goals and establish a starting point.	6 Consider personal, cultural, and linguistic factors.	7 Set reasonable objectives; provide appropriate materials and activities.	8 Search ESL Web sites for materials, lessons, and activities.	9 Use visual aids.	10 Use formal and informal means of assessment.	11 Identify the students' problems; seek help for specific needs.	12 Use simple self-assessment procedures.
Assessment/testing	✓			✓						✓		✓
Content areas	✓				✓		✓	✓	✓	✓		✓
Culture	✓	✓				✓						
Language skills												
Grammar	✓	✓	✓	✓	✓		✓	✓		✓	✓	✓
Listening	✓		✓								✓	✓
Speaking	✓		✓				✓		✓	✓	✓	✓
Reading	✓		✓	✓	✓		✓	✓	✓	✓	✓	✓
Writing	✓		✓	✓	✓		✓	✓	✓	✓	✓	✓
Pronunciation		✓	✓	✓			✓	✓		✓	✓	✓
Texts		✓										
Web sites								✓				

Discussions of language level and of adult and K–12 students are incorporated into all chapters.

Three Case Studies

Case Study 1: Four Somali Refugee Women

Fatima, Kherto, Halima, and her mother, Sharifa, are from Somalia. All are adult women, Sharifa in her early 40s and the other three women in their mid-20s. They had been in the United States for less than 4 months when they were resettled in their new homes through the sponsorship of Catholic Charities Refugee Resettlement Office. When they arrived, none of the women spoke English; they all use the Somali language at home. They exhibit no or very low literacy skills in their first language (L1) and through an interpreter have indicated that they did not attend school in Somalia.

Sharifa and Kherto are widows; the other two women are married. They all live in extended family units and hold specific roles within their families. They are in charge of buying and preparing food and seeing to the children's health and education. They are living in temporary housing and awaiting permanent facilities. The husbands of Halima and Fatima both work in a factory. The youngest woman, Kherto, has indicated that she wants to get a job eventually.

Although the women have not asked to learn English, they have stated that they wish to know how to shop, count money and calculate prices, and explain illnesses to the doctor. They are particularly concerned about knowing the names of foods containing pork, which is forbidden to them by their religion. They have not said that they want to learn to read; instead they have said they want to know how to write their names and to recognize signs and names of food.

When the women are told that English tutoring is available to them, they are at first reluctant to join a class. Eventually they do, but they sit in the back of the class and do not speak. After a week, the social workers suspect that the women will not participate in a class with men and ask for a female volunteer ESL tutor. The women are invited to tutoring sessions arranged for them by the Refugee Resettlement Office. They agree to come only after being assured that day care is available for their children and that transportation will be provided.

Within a short time, the women become very involved in the sessions and show an interest in the tutor and her family. They eventually receive 80 hours of tutoring. Afterward, several ask to join regular ESL classes.

✦ A 1-Hour Session

9:05 a.m.: The four Somali women enter the class a few minutes late because the van driver has been delayed in traffic. On the chalkboard, the tutor, Ms. Freeman, has written the following:

> Yesterday was Tuesday, October 14.
> Today is Wednesday, October 15.
> Tomorrow will be Thursday, October 16.

Ms. Freeman greets the students by saying, "Good morning." Halima and Fatima repeat the greeting. Kherto and Sharifa, Halima's mother, say nothing but simply nod their heads.

9:06 a.m.: The students settle into the desks, and some remove their veils. The tutor points to the calendar on the wall and says the sentence, "Today is Wednesday, October 15." She repeats this several times. Some of the students try to repeat after her. She asks everyone to repeat as a group. She then states, "Today is . . . ." Halima, responds, "Today is Wednesday." Ms. Freeman says, "Good!" She then states, "Yesterday was Tuesday, October 14," and crosses out the date on the calendar. All the dates up to October 14 have already been crossed out, a routine Ms. Freeman always follows.

9:10 a.m.: As a review, Ms. Freeman writes the numbers 1–20 on the board and says the name of each number as she writes it. The students repeat, some of them getting ahead of her to say the next number. The tutor then writes the numbers 20–50 on the board and says each. She practices the words *thirty, forty,* and *fifty* because the students seem comfortable with numbers 1–10. The students repeat several times. She then says a number and has a student point to it.

9:15 a.m.: Ms. Freeman gives each student a homemade Bingo card with various numbers from 1–50 written in the squares. She gives pennies to each student. She counts the pennies, and the students do the same. They then use the pennies as Bingo markers. She begins calling numbers, and she demonstrates the task by looking for each number she calls on her Bingo card and covering it with a penny if she finds it. If the number is not on the card, she gestures and says, "No." The students catch on quickly. They play one game in which Ms. Freeman calls the numbers, each time showing the students the numbers she calls. If the women have the numbers on their cards, they cover them. If they do not, they say or gesture "No." Finally, Kherto has covered a row of numbers, and Ms. Freeman points to it and says "Bingo!" She then gives Kherto a small piece of candy. The women laugh and clap and want to play again. Ms. Freeman plays again, this time not showing the numbers but allowing students to find them on their own. Halima helps her mother and translates into Somali.

Finally, Fatima covers a row of numbers, and Ms. Freeman points to it and says "Bingo!" She then gives Fatima a small piece of candy. The women want to play again.

9:25 a.m.: During the third game, the tutor goes around the room with an envelope containing little cards with numbers on them. Each of the women picks a number and says it. The women help each other by cueing those who are reluctant to respond. If no one knows, Ms. Freeman says the number, and everyone repeats. Each time someone says a number, everyone looks for the number to cover. Finally, Kherto wins again and puts her hand out for the candy. Everyone laughs, and Kherto gives the candy to her mother. They play one more time.

9:35 a.m.: Ms. Freeman gives each student a few more pennies. She takes her own pennies and counts them aloud. Finally, she announces, "I have 33 cents." She writes *$.33* on the board. She asks each student to count her own pennies, and all work at counting aloud while Ms. Freeman observes each one. Finally, she asks, "How much do you have? I have $.33." Each student responds, "I have $_____." Ms. Freeman then gives each woman a handout with the numbers 1–50 written on it, with blanks for some of the numbers (e.g., 1, 2, ___, 4, 5, 6, ___). She asks the students to read the numbers aloud and orally fill in the blanks. The students read together and complete the exercise. The tutor tells them to take the paper home and fill in the blanks if they know how to write the numbers. She says they will correct the papers next time.

9:45 a.m.: Ms. Freeman holds up a picture of a person with lines pointing to the head, the arms, the legs, the hands, and the feet. She points to the picture and repeats the vocabulary words several times. She then points to her own head, arms, legs, hands, and feet and says the words again. This time Halima and Fatima begin repeating after her. The tutor motions for the women to point to the picture as she says the words. All but Sharifa do so. Ms. Freeman repeats the activity, this time helping Sharifa point to the item. She then motions for the students to stand up. As she says each word, she points to each body part. The students follow her and point to each part of their own bodies. After repeating this several times, Ms. Freeman stops pointing to her own body but continues saying "head," "arm," "leg," "hand," and "foot," showing a card with the word on it as she says the word. The women continue pointing to their bodies, and the tutor praises their efforts by clapping.

9:55 a.m.: Ms. Freeman gives each student a picture of a person along with five labels, each with the name for a different body part written on it. She holds up one label, says "arm," and places the label on the picture in the correct spot. Each student looks for the label *arm* and holds it up. Ms. Freeman helps those having difficulty. The women repeat each name after Ms. Freeman says it, and they place each label in the correct spot. They then gather the labels and repeat the activity several times until each seems to understand the labeling exercise. Ms. Freeman indicates through gestures that they will learn more names for body parts next time.

10:00 a.m.: Ms. Freeman collects the pennies in a sack and says good-bye to everyone. She hands each student a piece of candy as they leave. The students all smile and say, "Bye. Tomorrow."

After the students leave, Ms. Freeman writes some observations in her journal:

Oct. 15 session

- reviewed numbers 1–20

- introduced numbers 20–50

- used Bingo for number recognition and to elicit verbal response; students responded well to candy reward

- began counting money using pennies and illustrated way to show money ($____)

- provided handout for continued work at home and for a quick check of progress of numbers

- introduced five body parts

- taught the words for body parts and did a word recognition exercise

She has a folder for each student with a checklist. For each student, she dates and checks the squares labeled *Numbers 1–20, Numbers 20–50*, and *Five Major Body Parts*, and writes comments, such as "recognizes and uses" or "recognizes only but repeats willingly."

Beside each student's name, she writes the date and a brief comment:

Halima 10/15—participates willingly; not afraid to speak; helps others

Sharifa 10/15—still reluctant to speak; relies on Halima—might still be in silent period; shows good recognition and uses gestures or actions to convey understanding

Fatima 10/15—participates willingly; good recognition and attempts at speaking; defers to Halima—must give her more opportunity to answer on her own

Kherto 10/15—seems to catch on quickly even though she missed the last class; enjoyed the Bingo game and loved winning; was eager to continue the activity

Case Study 2: A Boy From India

Omar is a 12-year-old boy from India. He came to the United States 2 years ago with his parents, older brother, and two younger sisters. All members of his family can speak English, the second language of most Indians, but they have some problems being understood when they speak to Americans. Omar and his siblings began learning British English in the first grade at age 7. At home they converse in the dialect of their native region in India. Omar's father runs a family grocery store in which he employs many of his relatives who came to the United States shortly after he did.

Omar's father calls the ESL department of a local university because he has heard that some good tutors who are earning a degree in ESL offer their services free of charge so they can get some teaching experience. Because he cannot afford to pay a professional tutor, he decides this is his best option for getting competent help for his son, who is failing English and social studies in the seventh grade and is having some social adjustment problems. When he calls the university, the director of the ESL department assigns him to a 23-year-old MA candidate named Marjory Hawkins, who asks for background information on Omar and his language needs.

When Omar's parents bring him to Ms. Hawkins' home for their session, he is accompanied by his mother, who is wearing a sari, and his father, in a business suit. Omar is wearing a pair of dress slacks and a button-down shirt. The mother proceeds to remove her shoes as they enter Ms. Hawkins' home. The family's formality surprises Ms. Hawkins, but she invites them into her home to sit down and get acquainted. She asks if they have any questions for her and assures them that she will do everything she can to help Omar. She then greets Omar with a warm, friendly smile and says she will try to make their time together enjoyable so that he will not miss spending time with his friends after school. She asks if he will be giving up the opportunity to play on any athletic teams. Omar says that he does not have any friends at school and that he does not play any sports. He just wants to get better grades. She asks the parents for permission to contact Omar's teachers to let them know they can call on her to help with problems they observe in the classroom. She then thanks the parents for coming and suggests that she and Omar get started right away; she asks the parents to return at 5:00 p.m.

◆ The First Tutoring Session

4:00 p.m.: Ms. Hawkins leads Omar to her tutoring office, which is really one corner of her den. Omar notices a magnetic dry-erase board standing on a table. There are two chairs side by side near the table and writing materials on the table. Ms. Hawkins invites Omar to sit down and tells him she is happy to meet him. She says she wants him to feel comfortable asking her any questions at all about what happens at school during classroom activities as well as social activities. She then tries to get to know him a little better by asking him, "What are your favorite subjects in school?" He responds that he loves math and science but hates English and social studies. When she asks why, he says that he likes to do things, not just sit there and listen to the teacher talk. In math and science students can go to the board and work on projects, but in English they diagram sentences or read stories, and in social studies they spend a lot of time reading their book aloud. When the teacher calls on him to read, the students laugh because they think he talks "funny." "Is that why you don't have any friends at school?" she asks. "Yes," says Omar, "and also because whenever I talk, they always ask me to repeat everything." She asks Omar to tell her what is most difficult for him in school. He says that he has trouble understanding the English and social studies teacher because she speaks very fast and uses words he does not understand. He never knows what to study for her tests. Ms. Hawkins then asks Omar what he likes to do when he has free time. He says he enjoys playing video games.

4:10 p.m.: Ms. Hawkins asks Omar to show her his textbooks in English and social studies. She makes a note of the titles and publishers. She then asks him if he has brought any of his old quizzes and tests with him. Before looking these over, she gives him a folder with her name and telephone number on the front. She asks Omar to get out a piece of paper from one of the inside pockets and gives him a pencil with an eraser; she asks him to write a paragraph about his favorite video game and why he likes it. She tells him not to worry about spelling and grammar but just to write whatever he wants to tell her. She sets a timer and tells him to write as much as he can in 5 minutes. Ms. Hawkins then photocopies the tests so she can evaluate them more fully later.

4:20 p.m.: The timer goes off, and Ms. Hawkins asks Omar to give her the paper. Then she asks Omar to talk to her about why he likes video games. She turns on her audiotape recorder and lets Omar practice saying simple things like his name and address. He thinks it is fun to hear his own voice played back to him. Now he is ready to begin talking on audiotape. He asks if he can listen to himself again. Ms. Hawkins says yes.

4:30 p.m.: Ms. Hawkins asks Omar if he has any quizzes, tests, or homework that he would like help with for the next day. He says he just has some homework in English: to read a story and answer some questions about it. Ms. Hawkins suggests that they look at the pictures first and then read the introduction and questions. The introduction says that the story is about a mother and her son. Before they start to read it, Ms. Hawkins asks if Omar has any idea what the story is about. Omar says it is about a mother and son walking in the woods when a forest fire breaks out. Because the story has a lot of dialogue, Ms. Hawkins and Omar play the parts of the two characters. They stand up and act out some of the things that the characters do in the story. Ms. Hawkins makes a mental note that Omar has difficulty saying final consonants and that he often places stress on the wrong syllable, but she never interrupts Omar to correct his pronunciation while they are reading the story aloud.

4:45 p.m.: When they finish the story, Ms. Hawkins asks Omar if he has any questions about it. He points at the words *consumed* and *smoldering,* which he had trouble pronouncing, and asks what they mean. Ms. Hawkins says the words for Omar and asks him to repeat them. She then suggests that they look at the words in the story to see if they can figure out what they mean before asking Omar to look up the words in the *Longman Dictionary of American English* (Stern, 1997). Ms. Hawkins then says that there is not enough time to write the answers to the questions but that they can talk about them. She would like to ask Omar to summarize the story for her in his own words, but because she has been asked to help him get better grades, she feels it is her responsibility to be sure he can handle the homework. Omar can answer the questions about the events of the story, but he has difficulty with questions that require inference and personal opinion.

4:59 p.m.: Ms. Hawkins asks Omar to bring his folder with him to their next session and to write down any questions he has on the paper she has provided. She tells him that he has done very well and that he should call her if he has any questions about his homework when he gets home. She asks Omar to give his teacher the Teacher Information Form (see chapter 3) and to bring it back to her at their next session.

◆ Follow-Up

After Omar leaves, Ms. Hawkins writes down some observations about his strengths and weaknesses in reading, writing, and pronunciation on his Student Information Card.

Weaknesses

- has trouble saying final -*d*, -*t*, and -*s*
- often places stress on wrong syllable in three- to four-syllable words
- in his writing, repeats words unnecessarily when he could use an adjective clause or a pronoun
- does not enunciate clearly when he is speaking or reading
- has difficulty with inference in reading

Strengths

- has good reading comprehension
- comprehends and follows directions well
- demonstrates strong motivation to improve

Special Observations

- enjoys working with an audiotape recorder
- prefers hands-on activities
- does not like to express his opinion

Case Study 3: A Woman From China

Kim Su Watson is from Beijing, China. She is 25 years old and has been in the United States for 7 years. She and her husband, a U.S. businessman who works for United Airlines, speak fluent Chinese, which is their language of communication at home. Kim Su has just completed her nursing degree from a local university.

Kim Su studied English in China for 10 years before coming to the United States. However, the primary emphasis was on grammar, reading, and translation with little opportunity to actually speak English. As a result of her studies and life in the United States, she understands English very well but still has difficulty making herself understood because of a strong Chinese accent and some habitual grammar problems. Although she was successful in her nursing studies at a U.S. university, she was too busy to interact socially with U.S. students.

Kim Su now wants to improve her spoken English to help her get a nursing position and to communicate better with her husband's business associates at social functions. She believes that all she needs is the opportunity to speak on a regular basis with a native U.S. speaker, so she and her husband decide to contact a local church that has trained volunteer tutors in ESL. Kim Su's husband calls the church, and he requests a female tutor who is older than his wife and can meet with her two or three times a week. The tutor learns that Kim Su's husband is happy that Kim Su wants to improve her English to function better as his wife at social events, but he does not want the tutor to spend too much time helping Kim Su get a job. He says they will probably start a family soon, and Kim Su will not need a job outside the home. He says she can practice her nursing skills on her own family.

Mr. Watson accompanies his wife when she meets the tutor, Ms. Rogers, at the church for the first time. Ms. Rogers greets the Watsons with a warm smile and introduces herself. Mr. Watson formally shakes hands with Ms. Rogers while his wife bows, and proceeds to inform her that his wife needs help with her conversation skills. Ms. Rogers asks Kim Su if she has ever taken English conversation classes. Kim Su smiles shyly and shakes her head to indicate "No" while her husband answers the question verbally. Ms. Rogers smiles again at the Watsons and says she will do everything she can to help Kim Su.

✦ The First 1-Hour Session

10:00 a.m.: Ms. Rogers leads Kim Su to a small classroom that is equipped with a blackboard. Ten student desks are arranged in two rows, and in the front of the room is a large teacher's desk with two chairs. Ms. Rogers invites Kim Su to sit in one of these chairs, and she sits in the other one. Kim Su attempts to say, "Thank you, Ms. Logers." Instead of correcting her pronunciation, Ms. Rogers asks Kim Su to call her "Amy." This time, Kim Su says, "Thank you, Ms. Amy." Ms. Rogers then asks, "What would you like me to call you?" Kim Su then replies, "Please call me Kim, like American students in nursing school." Ms. Rogers then hands Kim Su a folder and says, "Kim, please use this folder to keep the handouts I give you and bring it to class with you every time we meet. My name and telephone number are on the front in case you need to call me." Ms. Rogers observes that Kim Su appears less shy without her husband.

10:05 a.m.: Ms. Rogers turns on the audiotape recorder that is sitting on the desk and begins to speak slowly and clearly. "Kim Su, today I would like to get to know you a little better. I'm going to begin by asking you some questions about yourself." At first Kim Su appears nervous, but she relaxes when she realizes that the questions are easy to answer. For example, Ms. Rogers asks, "Kim, where are you from?" When Kim Su answers, "I from China," Ms. Rogers says, "What city? Can you show me on this map?" "I from Beijing, big city in China." Kim then locates Beijing on the map. The conversation continues as follows:

Ms. Rogers:	Did you learn to speak English in China?
Kim Su:	I learn to lead and lite, but not speak. I only speak when I meet husband and come to United States.
Ms. Rogers:	You must have done a lot of reading and writing in nursing school. Why did you decide to become a nurse?
Kim Su:	Because I rike to help people and I can always get job.
Ms. Rogers:	Did you speak to the teachers and the other students in your nursing classes?
Kim Su:	I sometime have to speak English to do special assignment.
Ms. Rogers:	What kind of assignments?
Kim Su:	To give speech about something we learn in class and to do group project.

10:15 a.m.: Ms. Rogers turns off the audiotape recorder. This interview and Kim Su's success in a U.S. nursing school convince Ms. Rogers that Kim Su understands English very well. Kim Su's speech contains grammar and pronunciation errors, but Ms. Rogers has little difficulty understanding when she listens carefully. She notes that Kim Su tends to speak softly and to look down when she speaks. There are several conversation books on the desk, and Ms. Rogers now selects one called *Well Said* (Grant, 2001) because it is designed for students like Kim Su, who can read, write, and understand English but have difficulty with effective communication due to pronunciation problems. She hands Kim Su a copy of the book and then reads part of the introduction, entitled "To the Student," aloud to Kim. This section explains the book's purpose and focus, and helps the student set realistic goals. After completing the reading, Ms. Rogers asks Kim Su if she has any questions. Kim Su asks if she will need any other books. Ms. Rogers says she will need a copy of the *Longman Dictionary of American English* (Stern, 1997) and gives her one.

10:20 a.m.: Ms. Rogers asks Kim Su to turn to Reading 1 in *Well Said* and to read it aloud. Kim Su asks if she can read silently first in case there are words she does not know. Ms. Rogers agrees, and she uses this time to write Kim Su's name and the date at the top of her copy of the reading. When Kim Su is ready, Ms. Rogers turns on the audiotape recorder. She underlines syllables and letters that Kim Su omits or mispronounces. She also places a stress mark over syllables that Kim Su incorrectly stresses. At the end of the reading Ms. Rogers writes the words *monotone, choppy,* and *soft voice.*

10:25 a.m.: Ms. Rogers now reads the same passage aloud. She then plays Kim Su's recorded reading back to Kim Su and asks her to underline her own mistakes. Kim Su points out that her voice does not sound smooth when she reads. Ms. Rogers observes that Kim Su has not underlined any of her other problems. Kim Su says, "What do you mean, underline?" Ms. Rogers explains and then says, "I'm sorry I did not make it clear to you. Please ask questions whenever you don't understand me. Let me play the recording again. I want you to become aware of your own pronunciation mistakes so that you can begin to work on them one at a time."

10:40 a.m.: When Kim Su is finished with the reading, Ms. Rogers does another short interview using questions on page 9 of *Well Said*. She continues to record Kim Su's responses to the following questions:

Ms. Rogers:	What is your purpose for studying English?
Kim Su:	To speak better English so people will not ask me to repeat what I say.
Ms. Rogers:	How much English do you speak every day?
Kim Su:	Maybe 5 minutes unless I out with my husband.
Ms. Rogers:	In what kinds of situations do you speak English?
Kim Su:	In grocery store, at parties with husband, at doctor's office, at post office.
Ms. Rogers:	What do you hope to achieve in this class?
Kim Su:	To get rid of Chinese accent and learn how to say English sounds better.

Ms. Rogers explains that she can help Kim Su speak more clearly so that Americans will understand her better, but she probably will not be able to get rid of her accent. In fact, Ms. Rogers says, Kim Su does not need to get rid of it to be understood. She also says that Kim Su will need to speak more English every day and offers to introduce Kim Su to some other women from the church who do not speak English as their L1.

10:45 a.m.: Ms. Rogers says she wants Kim Su to keep track of her own progress as she works on her speaking skills. She asks Kim Su to rate her present speaking skills on a scale of 1–6 as explained on page 14 of *Well Said*.

1   The listener understands only occasional words.

2   The listener requires constant repetition.

3   The listener is distracted by frequent variations that often prevent understanding.

4   Pronunciation variations distract the listener, but he/she usually understands.

5   Pronunciation variations rarely distract the listener who has no trouble understanding.

6   Pronunciation is almost like that of a native speaker with few isolated pronunciation errors.

Ms. Rogers asks where Kim Su thinks she is now on the scale. Kim Su says she is a 2. When Ms. Rogers asks where Kim Su would like to be at the end of the class, Kim Su says she wants to be at least a 4. Ms. Rogers says she can do that, but she will have to practice English every day. She offers to introduce her to some of the women at the church.

10:55 a.m.: Ms. Rogers tells Kim Su that their first class is almost over and asks her if she has any questions. Kim Su wants to know if there is any homework. Ms. Rogers asks her to look at Reading 2 in *Well Said* and to underline all words with a final *-s*. She models some of the words and asks Kim Su to repeat after her. She then asks Kim Su to practice the reading several times at home before recording it on audiotape and to concentrate only on saying the final *-s* sound.

11:00 a.m.: Mr. Watson arrives promptly and wants to know how the class has gone. Ms. Rogers explains that she and Kim Su have spent the first class evaluating Kim Su and that she has given Kim Su a speaking book and an ESL dictionary. She also recommends that Kim Su meet other women with whom she can practice her English. Mr. Watson agrees. Kim Su smiles happily at Ms. Rogers as she and her husband prepare to leave.

✦ Follow-Up

Ms. Rogers listens to the audiotape and writes the following observations on Kim's card:

Special Problems

- Language problems:
  - has trouble with initial *l/r* sounds
  - sometimes omits verb
  - usually uses simple present tense
  - sometimes omits *-s* on plural nouns
  - rarely uses *a, an, the*
- Cultural obstacles to English:
  - is reluctant to speak in front of husband
  - is reluctant to express opinions

Ms. Rogers then refers to *Learner English* (Swan & Smith, 2001) and discovers that these are predictable problems of native Chinese speakers.

Unit 1: Prepare

Many people view a tutor as someone who is an expert in a certain field but is not a real teacher. They think that a tutor waits for a student to arrive and then, on the spur of the moment, decides how to address the student's problem. The most successful tutors tell us that occasionally they have to teach spontaneously but that they follow certain procedures so that they are ready for anything the student needs. While searching the Internet for resources that ESL tutors could use, we discovered a list of 25 qualities that ESL students look for in a good teacher (Probst, 1999). Being consistently prepared was at the top of the list, second only to showing enthusiasm for the job and the subject. This unit will show how you can always be prepared by asking the right questions, gathering important tools, and following an organized format.

CHAPTER 1

"What do I do first?"

Gather information.

You have agreed to tutor an ESL student but feel a bit lost. What should you do first? The answer is simple: You need to gather various types of information that will eventually help you prepare to tutor your student.

First, you need personal information about your student—telephone number, address, name of parent or sponsoring agency—in case you need to contact your student for a last-minute change in tutoring time or place. This information also allows you to communicate with a parent, spouse, family member, or sponsoring agency about the student's progress.

Second, you should know something about the student's background. How old is your student? What is the student's native language? Can the student read and write in the native language or any other languages? How long has the student studied English? If currently residing in the United States, how long has the student been there? What is the highest level of education attained? Is the student working toward any particular goals? Are there any special problems that may interfere with language acquisition?

One means of gathering this information is to ask the student or the student's parent or sponsor to help you complete a Student Information Card similar to the one shown in Figure 1 (and included as a reproducible form at the end of this chapter). In this chapter we explain how to use the information you gather.

Figure 1. Student Information Card

Name: *Kim Duc Lo*

Preferred first name: *Kim*   Date: *8/12/02*

Name of parents, sponsoring agency, or contact person: *Mr. Wong Lo*

Address: *1225 Murphy Avenue*

Telephone: *555-3999*   Age: *16*

Grade: *10*   School (if appropriate): *Elliston High*

Native language: *Korean*

Other languages (spoken or written): *English*

Years of English study: *3*   Length of time in the United States (if applicable): *4*

Highest level of education: *11th grade in Korea (note: placed in 10th grade at local high school)*

Special goals: *to pass sophomore English and improve writing*

Special problems: *has trouble organizing paragraphs and essay; grammar—can't recognize sentence fragments*

Age

Knowing the student's age helps you make two important decisions: (a) what to teach and (b) how to teach.

✦ Young Children

Very young children, ages 3–6, generally do not require individual tutoring. Instead, they acquire social language by interacting with other children in day care and preschool and use that language as a basis for building beginning literacy skills. However, some 5- to 7-year-olds may need tutoring to acquire prereading and reading skills.

Tutoring sessions for young children should be short, should include a variety of activities to accommodate short attention spans, and should focus on learning by doing. Young children learn through play and physical activity. Also, they pay more attention to the functions of language than to its forms. You should therefore engage young students in various activities as they listen and respond to language. You might have them react to stories, role-play, draw pictures, or simply respond to commands (e.g., "Show me the letter *B*"; "Pick up the truck, not the red fire engine"; "Can you tell me what happens next in the story?").

Correcting the grammar of very young children is an exercise in futility. Young children learn grammar inductively; that is, with their first language (L1) and any subsequent languages, they figure it out from what they hear and make generalizations about how the language works. Do not provide young students with grammar explanations. Modeling correct forms works much better.

✦ Older Children

Older, school-aged children (ages 7–18) may need tutoring to help them develop literacy skills and pass academic subjects. In fact, you may be asked to use the student's school texts in the tutoring sessions, the sessions themselves may revolve around the school topics, and you will want to maintain contact with the classroom teacher to discuss progress.

If you tutor school-aged children in English, you may be teaching English in the context of the school subject, and the academic subject becomes the text of the lesson. You are still a language tutor, however. Focus on content and on the language of the academic subject, paying careful attention to whether the student recognizes and uses vocabulary and structures that are important for the school subjects. Make sure the student understands and responds to the words and concepts used for math, geography, English literature, art, and other subjects.

✦ Adults

Adult ESL students fall into various categories depending on their educational level and purpose for learning English. Some newly arrived immigrants and refugees, for example, learn survival English. Their goal is to communicate in English to fulfill basic needs, such as shopping, locating housing, and getting a job. They may or may not be literate in their native language, but they need some basic literacy skills in English in order to read road signs, warning labels, and important documents, such as job application forms. You should determine the most immediate needs of such students and begin by addressing them. Texts that outline survival English topics are readily available; some are listed in Appendix A.

> If the adult students are not literate, you will want to teach some word recognition skills along with social language and survival English. Eventually, the students may want to learn to read, and these early experiences of learning social language and survival English will become the basis for early literacy.

Tutors teach adults best by focusing on adult topics and using pictures, gestures, and role playing, and adults learn best when they are motivated to learn by lessons that are relevant, interesting, and appropriate (see Figure 2 for more important points on teaching adult learners). Realia—objects from the real world, such as newspaper grocery ads or job application forms—make the tutoring sessions helpful and practical.

Some intermediate- or advanced-level adults seek tutoring for special purposes. They may be professionals who want to become more fluent in conversational English for job purposes. They may need the help of a native speaker in editing papers they have written, or they may

Tutors who are unprepared to work around cultural differences or who are unaware of such differences will soon experience frustration. A distinct benefit of tutoring ESL is the opportunity to meet people from different backgrounds and learn about their culture from them. Use those opportunities to your advantage, and apply them to the tutoring sessions.

Length of English Study

Although length of language study is not always an indicator of language skill, it is nonetheless a beginning point for you. You might, for example, make some decisions about the type of assessment to use once you know the student's age and number of years of English study.

Sometimes students who indicate many years of English study remain at the beginning or low intermediate stage of listening and speaking. Those students, however, often demonstrate very good reading and writing skills and possess a good background in structure or grammar. If you can determine that in your assessment (see chapter 4), you can eventually use that background as a basis for lessons.

Students who indicate they have no background in English may actually be *false beginners*, that is, they have a minimal background but do not feel comfortable in their knowledge and wish to start again. They soon become bored, however, as they relearn language features they already know. You will soon detect this and may have to adjust lessons appropriately, incorporating a quick review of English structures before moving to more advanced-level study. Of course, true beginners exist, but they should not be confused with false beginners.

Years in the United States

Knowing how long the student has been in the United States will help you make several decisions. A student who has just arrived may have immediate language needs growing out of the need to adjust and adapt. Motivation may be high, and you can use that to your advantage. You will want to advise the student of opportunities for using English and understanding spoken English (e.g., the use of closed captions on television shows).

The student who has been in the United States for some time may feel frustration at not having mastered English yet. That student may have developed routines that hinder language acquisition (e.g., depending on a child for translation or avoiding situations in which English is required). You will need to know the daily routine of this student to determine when language skills are required.

Highest Level of Education

Knowing the student's educational background is very important in determining the kinds of activities you choose and the demands you place on the student. Highly educated students are often quick to understand grammar points, comprehend what they read, and attempt various types of writing. They may prefer materials that appeal to their knowledge and background. These students often like to be challenged, and they may feel insulted if the materials appear too simplistic.

The student who indicates limited schooling on the Student Information Card presents different problems. You will want to teach this student language skills along with some content. For example, as you teach numbers, you may wish to use them to teach simple arithmetic. From there you may move to balancing a checkbook, an immediate practical application. This student will use language skills to learn and acquire new information.

Special Goals, Special Problems

Students sometimes indicate a particular goal for the tutoring they seek. Some want help passing one of the standardized tests of language skills required to get into school or be hired by a company. Most colleges and universities, for example, require nonnative English speakers to take the Test of English as a Foreign Language (TOEFL) for admission, and some companies or corporations require the Test of English for International Communication (TOEIC) of international applicants. Students may indicate a need for tutoring in order to pass the TOEFL or TOEIC. Fortunately for the tutor, study guides for these tests and other, similar tests are readily available. If you are tutoring a student who needs to pass standardized language tests, focus on the skills tested in those and other examinations.

Students sometimes exhibit special problems for tutors. Students whose native language does not use the Roman alphabet (i.e., the ABCs), such as Japanese, Arabic, or Russian, may need to work on the reading and writing of that alphabet. Some students may exhibit auditory or speech problems, and you may have to ask the student to be evaluated by a speech pathologist or audiologist first to rule out speech pathology problems or hearing loss. Note on your Student Information Card any other problems you detect in your first few sessions. If the problems are severe, such as obvious speech pathology problems, you may decide to discontinue tutoring, refer the student for professional help, or both.

You can also use the Student Information Card or a dossier kept on the student to make observational notes. You might note, for example, particular and persistent problems in pronunciation. You will also want to note and date evidence of progress being made. It may be helpful to indicate whether the student responds better to some activities than to others. As you make notes for future reference and adapt the lessons for your student, you appeal to the student's learning style and individualize your lessons, one of the benefits of tutoring over classroom study.

Case Studies: Points of Interest

✦ Case Study 1

- Ms. Freeman has been chosen to be the tutor because of her interest in tutoring and her skills and because the agency has requested a female tutor.

- For the Somali women, Ms. Freeman decides to plan all lessons around survival English topics and has already asked a translator from the Refugee Resettlement Office to determine from the women the topics they want to learn.

- Ms. Freeman decides to focus on oral skills but also to teach the students to recognize some important words, such as *stop, don't walk,* and *danger.* Later, she will show them how to identify food in cans and containers by recognizing food words. She plans to teach body parts and words for illnesses in case the women need to see any health care specialists.

- Ms. Freeman uses as much realia as she can, such as newspaper ads for grocery items, catalogues with clothing pictures, and cooking utensils.

- When Ms. Freeman notices that the women respond well to rewards, she notes that in her journal and plans to use more activities like the Bingo numbers game.

- Ms. Freeman is careful to establish a routine for each session. The women are still at a low beginning level of language use and come to rely on knowing what to do in class because of the routines they follow each time.

✦ Case Study 2

- Omar, a middle-school-aged child, speaks and reads English but has difficulty with the school subjects that rely heavily on the reading and comprehension of text.

- Omar is not literate in his L1, so Ms. Hawkins plans to use the school texts to prepare the tutoring sessions and practice the specific skills he needs for English and social studies.

- She designs her tutoring session to include a variety of activities that move from writing, to speaking, to playing roles.

- She does not spend too much time on any one activity and uses a timer to make sure Omar works within time limitations. The fact that Omar can see a beginning and an end to the activity helps him set personal boundaries.

- Ms. Hawkins is aware that it is Omar's parents, not Omar, who have sought tutoring. She realizes that this could be a problem. Student success often depends on the motivation of the student, not the parents. Encouraging Omar by making the sessions enjoyable and having him succeed in small steps each time keeps him interested and stimulated.

- Ms. Hawkins makes each session comfortable and reassuring for Omar. Eventually, he begins to see progress as he understands more and more of his subject matter. When that happens, Omar gains confidence in his language ability.

✦ Case Study 3

- Kim Su has a specific goal for learning English—to communicate well with others socially.

- She is a professional who has already passed her nursing exams in English, so her reading and writing skills are well advanced. Not having much time to speak English with native speakers might eventually hamper her professionally, however, and she is aware of this.

- Although Kim Su's husband has encouraged her to pursue tutoring, his goals for her are different from her own. (Ms. Rogers finds herself in the middle of a conflict in purpose and must proceed carefully.) Ms. Rogers can respond to the goals of both husband and wife by designing sessions that allow Kim Su to communicate successfully in a variety of settings.

- The language sessions will proceed in a relaxed and informal manner, focusing on accurate pronunciation that allows for effective communication.

Student Information Card

Name: _____

Preferred first name: _____ Date: _____

Name of parents, sponsoring agency, or contact person: _____

Address: _____

Telephone: _____ Age: _____

Grade: _____ School (if appropriate): _____

Native language: _____

Other languages (spoken or written): _____

Years of English study: _____

Length of time in the United States (if applicable): _____

Highest level of education: _____

Special goals: _____

_____

Special problems: _____

_____

CHAPTER 2

"What materials should I have on hand?"

Acquire frequently used tutoring tools.

As an efficient, well-prepared tutor, you need to have a selection of texts, supplies, and equipment readily available to facilitate the teaching of all language skills. For example, the basic tutoring classroom, whether portable or fixed, should include an erasable board for you to write on, appropriate texts for the various language skills and levels of your students, stimulating visual aids, audiotapes featuring a variety of speakers, and writing materials for the student.

You may already possess (or can easily make) many of these items, and you can purchase texts and audiotapes at a minimal cost. If you plan to be an itinerant tutor, simply buy smaller models of some of the suggested items so that everything you need fits easily into a standard-sized briefcase. Following is a more detailed description of materials you may wish to acquire (see also the reproducible shopping list at the end of this chapter).

> Remember to save your receipts for all business purchases because such expenses may be tax deductible.

Classroom Supplies

Classroom supplies you might have on hand include

- a freestanding blackboard or dry-erase board—one of the most important tools. If the board is magnetized, you can also attach magnetized visual aids or manipulatives to it.
- writing tools, such as chalk, pens, pencils, felt-tip markers, and dry-erase pens
- a board eraser and correction fluid
- a notebook folder with pockets for handouts and work completed in your sessions. Attach your business card to the front of the folder, or simply write your name and telephone number on the cover, in case a student needs to call to cancel a class.
- a stapler for organizing handouts related to the same topic
- looseleaf paper for writing activities
- small (3-in.-by-5-in.) index cards to create flash cards with words or pictures
- large (5-in.-by-8-in.) index cards to record important information about your students. These can be filed easily in an index card box for future reference. If index cards are beyond your budget, you can make your own out of construction paper.
- a day planner, lesson planner, and address book. You can assemble your own inexpensively by purchasing a small looseleaf binder and 5-in.-by-8-in. paper.
- divider tabs for the binder. Write the student's name on the tabs, and use them to keep lesson plans for each student separate. When the student ends lessons with you, move those lessons to the back of the binder. If the student later calls you to resume lessons, you will have a valuable record of your work.

Electronic Equipment

An audiotape player is essential for teaching listening and speaking skills and for providing the student with the opportunity to hear the accents of various speakers of English. You should also have an extension cord or extra batteries on hand as well as blank audiotapes to record the progress of your students. A good AM-FM radio and audiotape player combination can be a useful, inexpensive purchase.

Another invaluable piece of equipment, which is a bit costly but soon pays for itself, is a small copier. Toner cartridges may be somewhat expensive but usually supply 1,000 copies or more. Remember that using your own copier is still far less expensive than taking handouts to someone else to copy. In addition, carrying copies is much easier than carrying full-size texts in a portable classroom.

If possible, use a computer with access to an Internet service provider. The Internet can provide the student with many ready-to-use ESL lessons that are graded online. If you commute to your student's home but cannot afford many of the classroom supplies and equipment, ask your student to provide as many as possible.

Reference Books

You can be an effective tutor without a huge library, but it is essential to have a dictionary and grammar book appropriate for the level of your students and a text that can be used to teach every level of the language skills that you wish to teach (see Figure 1 for tips on choosing an ESL textbook). The texts we mention here represent a sample collection for teaching ESL students of various ages and abilities. Additional resources can be found in Appendix A.

> Although you can create many of your own materials and use household items in your lessons, the inclusion of a reputable text adds credibility to your teaching methods. You do not need to obtain all of the suggested texts and materials at once, only those you need. Local ESL teachers may have materials they are willing to share with you or give to you.

✦ Vocabulary and Grammar Texts

Advise your students to use an ESL dictionary designed especially for their language needs. *The Oxford Picture Dictionary* (Shapiro & Adelson-Goldstein, 1998) is an excellent resource for beginning- and low intermediate–level students of all ages. A software version, The New Oxford Picture Dictionary CD-ROM (1997) is also available, along with workbooks containing exercises for each picture. For high intermediate– and advanced-level speakers, the *Longman Dictionary of American English* (Stern, 1997) provides easy-to-understand definitions, grammar explanations, pictures, and exercises.

Figure 1. How to Choose an ESL Textbook

> Using a good textbook can make tutoring easier for you and your student by providing structure, continuity, and reinforcement. To choose an appropriate text, look for the following features:
> - visual aids such as pictures, graphs, and charts
> - highlighting of important vocabulary in each chapter
> - vocabulary reinforcement activities in each chapter
> - an outline of the contents of each chapter
> - a gradual increase in difficulty as the book progresses
> - comprehension questions or activities at the end of each chapter
> - more visuals and less text for beginning-level students
> - a large, legible font
> - appropriate subject matter, language, and approach for your student's age and level

Longman's Azar Grammar Series is popular with many teachers and students because each grammar rule is clearly summarized in a chart for easy reference. Although the focus is on grammar, the series includes activities that develop writing and conversation skills. Prentice-Hall Regents' Side by Side series uses guided conversation to teach grammar and communication skills to beginning- and intermediate-level students.

✦ Pronunciation and Speaking Texts

Pronunciation is taught most effectively when combined with the teaching of other skills. Speakers of all ages and levels enjoy practicing English vocabulary, grammar, and pronunciation by reciting Graham's *Jazz Chants* (1978, 2001) and *Small Talk* (1986), which enable students to imitate the stress and intonation of English through music. *Pronunciation Pairs* (Baker & Goldstein, 1990) uses games, dialogues, and other listening/speaking activities to help beginning- and intermediate-level students develop American English pronunciation skills. *Well Said* (Grant, 2001) comes with a text and audiotape that offer practical suggestions to help more advanced-level, adult speakers of English improve their oral communication and pronunciation skills. *A Conversation Book: English in Everyday Life* (Carver & Fotinos, 1997) helps students who range from the beginning to the intermediate level learn to conduct two-way conversations and group discussions.

> You can get the names of ESL texts and their ISBNs from the Web sites of ESL publishers or from an online bookstore. You can order many of the resources mentioned here from a local commercial or college bookstore or from a Web site (see Appendix C).

✦ Integrated Series

Some textbook series teach all language skills in an integrated fashion. For example, McGraw-Hill's Interactions and Mosaics series consist of communicative texts for high school– and college-age students from the high beginning to the advanced level in grammar, reading, writing, and listening/speaking. The series has four texts for each level, each text focusing on one language skill but including activities that involve all language skills. For example, if a chapter in the grammar book uses vocabulary related to education, then so does the corresponding chapter in the reading, writing, and listening/speaking texts. Thus each text reinforces the vocabulary and language skills of the other three texts. Steck-Vaughn's Real-Life English, another integrated series, includes audiotapes. These texts are designed for students in Grade 8 through adults who range in level from preliteracy to intermediate.

For adult learners, the LifePrints and Laubach Way to English series (published by New Readers Press) teach language for surviving in an English-speaking environment, finding a job, and becoming a citizen. The series include texts and audiotapes in three levels from low beginning to intermediate. You can obtain teacher's manuals with suggested strategies for all of the above texts to make your job easier.

The Rosetta Stone (2000) is a popular software program designed for all ages and levels. Students learn many language skills and can progress at their own pace. PBS Adult Learning Service's *Crossroads Café* (2001) television series contains 26 half-hour episodes for many levels, all using real-life situations. It has been shown on the Library Channel and at the time of writing was soon to be available on videotape.

✦ Cultural References

To understand more about the native cultural and linguistic factors that may affect your student, you can refer to texts such as *Learner English* (Swan & Smith, 2001). This text explains the grammatical, phonetic, and behavioral features of language speakers from around the world and predicts specific problems that speakers from different areas might encounter when learning English. You can also purchase flyers called *Culturegrams* (2001), which give brief descriptions of the language, history, culture, and customs of people from more than 150 countries. These informative publications can be purchased individually or in bulk.

> Many texts that are not labeled *ESL* can be good for ESL students if they follow the guidelines listed in Figure 1.

Common Household Items

You may already have some of the best teaching aids in your home. For example, games such as Pictionary, Outburst, and Bingo are excellent for relaxing the student; are easy to explain and play; and are useful for teaching vocabulary, verb tenses, and numbers, for example.

You can use the pictures and the articles in magazines and newspapers to create lessons for every language skill. Some newspapers in large cities offer booklets with sample lesson plans to teach reading comprehension and other skills. You can create your own picture dictionary by collecting pictures from advertisements, coupons, and catalogues.

Teach your students how to shop for food and order in restaurants by using cookbooks that contain pictures of food items and by collecting menus from various restaurants. In some cities, restaurant delivery services (e.g., Takeout Taxi) provide a complimentary booklet of menus and prices from the various restaurants.

The teaching possibilities with ordinary objects are endless. For example, you can

- teach a student how to tell time by creating a clock with a cardboard package liner, a straight pin, a felt-tip marker, and cellophane tape
- teach a beginning-level student how to write numbers and letters by using a child's discarded writing book with upper- and lowercase letters of the alphabet written in both manuscript and cursive

- teach students how to read the directions and warnings on medicine bottles
- teach the alphabet and numbers by using a telephone directory
- teach telephone listening skills by asking students to call the time operator to get the current date, time, and temperature
- use a calendar to teach students to read and write days of the week, the numbers 1–31, and the date

Community Resources

Many free or inexpensive resources available within your own community can become teaching materials for all language skills within the tutorial setting. Adult students can benefit from, for example, application forms for a job, a Social Security card, a driver's license, a credit card, a library card, or a bank account. You use them much as you would a textbook. An added benefit of these resources is that they not only help students increase their language skills but also teach something about how to function within the community.

To find such materials, look in local libraries, bookstores, and toy and game stores, and ask literacy councils, commercial businesses, and government agencies. Even the television can provide free materials for language acquisition, and the Internet is an especially good source of materials, including lesson plans, exercises, and readings (see chapter 8).

✦ Libraries

The local public library is a wellspring of resources. Public libraries often carry a variety of ESL texts for various levels and needs as well as bilingual reading matter. In addition, libraries carry many complimentary resources that are helpful to ESL tutors, such as tax forms, housing information, and other government forms that an adult student might need. Other resource materials include instruction manuals to prepare international students for standardized tests such as the Test of English as a Foreign Language (TOEFL©) and the Test of Spoken English (TSE©).

Librarians are often familiar with textbooks designed for instructing ESL students in grammar, reading, and writing, and may also direct you to *high/low* reading materials (i.e., materials that are of high interest to adults but are written at a low level of English for easy comprehension). You can often borrow videotapes from libraries for a nominal fee. The reference section, of course, has newspapers and magazines from which you can select and copy articles appropriate to your students' needs and interests.

> Many libraries have space available for tutors to meet with students who are unable or unwilling to meet in a private home.

✦ Bookstores

Commercial bookstores carry instruction manuals for ESL students who are preparing for the TOEFL©, the TSE©, and other standardized tests. In addition, bookstores offer a selection of dictionaries especially designed for ESL students (see the list of dictionaries in Appendix A). If you cannot find a book but know the title, author, and publisher or the ISBN, a bookstore can order it at your request. The store may also carry books that list free materials and how to obtain them.

If your local bookstore cannot obtain the books you need, check with a local university bookstore, which may have used books for sale at reasonable prices. One advantage to shopping at a university store is that books are usually organized according to the English level of prospective college ESL students. In addition, employees of a college bookstore may be more familiar with ESL materials than employees of a commercial bookstore.

✦ Toy and Game Stores

As mentioned in chapter 2, toys and games help students relax and enjoy practicing communication skills in English:

- Use a doll or toy for role playing with elementary school students.
- Consider purchasing a deck of cards and a book of rules for such games as Old Maid or Go Fish, which make your student practice asking questions.
- Play Wheel of Fortune or Hangman, using words your student knows.
- As mentioned, Pictionary, Outburst, and Bingo are great icebreakers with students of all ages who are not ready to communicate orally but who have some knowledge of vocabulary.

Almost any word game or guessing game can be adapted to the proficiency level of an ESL student. If you are working with a small group, have one of the students explain the rules of a game to the other students. If working one-on-one, have your student teach you how to play a game from that student's native country.

✦ Literacy Councils

Most cities have a literacy council that offers free instruction to people who wish to become literate in English. Some councils sponsor organizations such as Laubach Literacy or Literacy Volunteers of America (see Appendix D). These organizations can meet some of the needs of nonnative speakers of English and may even offer a complimentary training program for prospective ESL tutors. From such agencies you can often obtain teacher education manuals with detailed lesson plans, dictionaries, texts, and activities for your student at a reasonable cost.

✦ Local Businesses

The materials you get from businesses bring realia—real-world items, such as flyers, brochures, pamphlets, applications, and maps—to the tutoring sessions. With these free materials, you can plan lessons on such topics as getting a job; taking prescription drugs correctly; opening and depositing money in a bank account; writing a check; filling out a job application; shopping for sale items; and becoming familiar with local museums, zoos, parks, and other places of entertainment. Place these collectibles in separate large, labeled manila envelopes so they will be easy to locate when you need them.

- A local travel agent may have a city map you can use to teach your student how to give and receive directions. The agent will also be glad to give you travel brochures with pictures and descriptions of popular attractions and airline schedules to help teach your students learn how to read timetables and prices. Some travel agencies even provide travel videotapes.

- Banks provide customers and visitors with materials such as deposit slips, forms for opening accounts and securing loans, and information on buying automobiles and houses.

- Drugstores give customers flyers on the appropriate use of prescription drugs and materials designed to educate the public on health issues.

- The post office has forms for sending packages, notifying the postal service of a change of address, or sending a postal money order.

- Department stores provide sale flyers that can be a good source of material for an individual picture dictionary that labels clothes, appliances, furniture, and household items. These stores also provide job application forms for potential employees and credit card application forms for customers.

- Grocery store flyers that advertise weekly specials often provide visual representations of grocery items and always list prices.

- Your local Visitors and Convention Bureau and Chamber of Commerce have materials designed to familiarize new arrivals with the local community and its entertainment and business offerings.

✦ Government Agencies

The federal government publishes more material than any other private or public agency does, much of it free and available to the public. The topics of pamphlets, brochures, and other informational materials include, for example, arranging a government mortgage loan or visiting a national park. Many libraries are repositories for government documents, and a quick search on the Internet will help you locate materials that are free of charge.

> The federal government (and many state education agencies) publishes helpful materials for low-literacy populations and those who are learning English. Your librarian can help you locate such items.

The state educational agency in your area also offers many useful resources. *State Education Agencies* (2002), part of the U.S. Department of Education's *Education Resource Organizations Directory*, at http://www.ed.gov/Programs/bastmp/SEA.htm, lists agencies that can give you "information, resources, and technical assistance on educational matters to the schools and the residents" (n.p.).

✦ Television

Television is a particularly good medium for language learning, particularly listening, because it presents language with visual cues.

- Shows that encourage language development provide interesting "homework" for your students.

- The many children's shows that encourage native-English-speaking children to develop literacy are helpful for young learners of ESL, too.

- Literate adults can benefit from watching close-captioned television, which allows adults to make a strong tie between what they see and what they hear.

- Any show that takes the viewer through a step-by-step process is helpful. Cooking shows, home improvement shows, and animal or safari adventure shows present language within an immediate context and are highly motivating for adults.

In conclusion, if you gather and organize the materials you need in the above five categories, you will be able to construct many commonly needed and requested ESL lessons, as illustrated in Case Studies: Points of Interest below.

Case Studies: Points of Interest

✦ Case Study 1

- Ms. Freeman has chosen materials that allow her to plan numerous beginning-level lessons.

- Her materials can be used in real-life situations.

- She uses manipulatives and realia (e.g., coupons, pennies, newspaper ads) because they help beginning-level students acquire language faster.

- She uses Bingo as a way to enhance interest and motivation in learning numbers.

- She will use complimentary coupons and flyers obtained from her local grocery store to teach the women the shopping skills they have requested

✦ Case Study 2

- Ms. Hawkins places the responsibility to bring materials on Omar, but she is still prepared with materials of her own in case he forgets to bring what she has requested.

- She has her audiotape recorder, audiotape, and copy machine available at all times to use for backup activities.

- She requests copies of Omar's textbooks and a syllabus of his classes to keep on hand for future lessons.

- She plans to obtain supplementary materials from the local library and the Internet to help Omar with social studies.

- A local travel agent has offered to give her complimentary maps and brochures on any country she desires.

- She will ask Omar to teach her how to play a video game to develop his speaking and social skills in English.

✦ Case Study 3

- Ms. Rogers knows that Kim Su wants to work on pronunciation, but she is not sure exactly what Kim Su needs.

- Ms. Rogers prepares by having her audiotape player and an audiotape available. She has also selected a text with analysis aids and practical oral activities for social and professional settings.

- She purchased a secondhand copy of *Well Said* (Grant, 2001) after talking to a well-informed sales person at a local university bookstore who knew that it was popular with ESL instructors and students.

- She plans to recommend that Kim Su watch soap operas or reruns of shows such as *The Cosby Show*, which feature clear, typical family dialogue.

Observe and Reflect

1. Make a list of the materials you will need to begin tutoring and the places where you can obtain them.

2. Make a budget for the money you are prepared to spend on materials.

3. Make a list of materials you can obtain from the Internet (see chapter 8) and other complimentary sources.

4. Using items such as bus and movie schedules, create questions to help your student gather information.

5. Choose books and magazines on topics of interest to your student to stimulate an interest in reading.

Shopping List

- ✦ Classroom Supplies
    - blackboard or dry-erase board
    - chalk, pens, pencils, felt-tip markers, dry-erase pens
    - board eraser, correction fluid
    - notebook folders
    - stapler
    - looseleaf paper
    - index cards (3-in. by 5-in. and 5-in. by 8-in.)
    - day planner, lesson planner, address book
    - tabbed dividers

- ✦ Electronic Equipment
    - audiotape player/recorder
    - audiotapes
    - extension cord
    - batteries
    - copier
    - computer and Internet access

- ✦ Reference Books
    (See Appendix A or chapter 2 for suggestions.)
    - dictionary
    - grammar text
    - pronunciation text
    - conversation text
    - integrated text
    - cultural background text

- ✦ Miscellaneous Items
    - games
    - magazines, newspapers, catalogues
    - cookbooks
    - menus
    - telephone directory
    - calendar
    - application forms (e.g., job, bank account, credit card)
    - maps
    - travel brochures
    - airline schedules

CHAPTER 3

"How should I structure my tutoring sessions?"

Follow an organized format.

Put yourself in the student's shoes for a moment, and consider these two scenarios.

- *Scenario 1:* You are visiting a tutor for your first session on making business presentations. When you enter the tutor's home, there is clutter everywhere. The tutor leads you to a kitchen table that is piled high with newspapers and books. As you sit down, a young child tears through the room and climbs onto the tutor's lap. Someone is in the kitchen rinsing off dishes and putting them in the dishwasher. The telephone rings, and, as the tutor gets up to answer it, the child cries for more attention. Five minutes have elapsed, and the $30-an-hour lesson has not yet begun. As you sit there waiting for the tutor to return, you observe that there is no evidence of any materials or plan related to the needs that you explained to the tutor the night before on the telephone. How does this scenario affect your confidence in the tutor?

- *Scenario 2:* You enter the tutor's home for your first tutoring session in how to write a résumé. The tutor is dressed neatly in casual business attire and greets you by name with a friendly handshake. The tutor then guides you to her office, which is really a corner of her family room. As you both enter the room, she closes the door and turns on an overhead light. There are no distracting sounds from a television or stereo. You notice that there is a round table with two chairs placed so that you and the tutor can easily look at each other as well as at a dry-erase board. When the tutor invites you to sit down in the chair on the right, you see that there is a folder and an index card with a pencil at your place. On the board the tutor has written the words *Employment Objective, Education,* and *Experience.* What is your first impression of this tutor?

Part of the organized tutoring format involves providing a good work space that tells the student that you are professional, you have a plan, and you know what you are doing. The tutor in Scenario 1 does nothing to convey seriousness of purpose to the student. However, the tutor in Scenario 2 is professional in appearance, behavior, and preparation. If you are tutoring away from home, you must still be concerned about providing a good work space. Wherever you go—a home, a school, a church, a volunteer agency—ask for a space that has privacy, good lighting, a table where two can sit side-by-side, and access to an electrical outlet. Many public libraries have soundproof rooms available for tutors.

ESL students often feel more comfortable if they know what to expect when they come to class, especially if they are at a beginning level and do not have the vocabulary or grammar structures to ask questions. In this chapter we present a five-part format that works in almost any tutoring situation.

> Not all tutoring situations are ideal. If you work in a school, you may not always be able to work in the same place, or you may have to share your tutoring place with another teacher. If you go to the student's house, you may encounter noise and interruptions over which you have no control. Your student may forget the materials you were counting on to conduct your lesson.

Step 1: Interview the Student

- During the first session, use the Student Information Card shown in chapter 1 to get information about students and to evaluate their listening and speaking skills. In addition to the information listed on the card, ask the students about their hobbies, special interests, or job experiences. Use this information to select supplementary materials that will interest the students.

- In subsequent sessions, ask the students if they have any problems, questions, or assignments that need to be addressed that day. Reassure your students that there is no such thing as a bad question in your sessions together and that you encourage questions at any time. Students from some countries may be reluctant to question you; in some cultures questioning the teacher is considered disrespectful.

Step 2: Review Old Material

- If the student is coming to you to develop personal language skills (i.e., reading, writing, grammar, listening/speaking) and you have chosen the texts, review the previous lesson by going over a homework assignment or exercise. If the student was reluctant to tell you about a problem with the last lesson, you can detect and address it here.

- If the student is coming to you to improve performance in an academic subject, go over quiz or test questions that were troublesome. Some teachers will not let their tests out of the classroom, so your student may need to write down difficult questions in a notebook. You can let teachers know that you are available to help their student by asking your student to give them a Teacher Information Form (included as a reproducible form at the end of this chapter).

Step 3: Introduce New Material

- Introducing new material involves the presentation of a lesson plan. Below are general formats to use for various lesson plans. (See chapter 7 for detailed instructions on planning lessons that follow these formats.) Listing the activities of the lesson plan on the dry-erase board and checking them off as they are accomplished is helpful to you as well as to the student.

- Occasionally, the student may ask you to help with an assignment or with test preparation instead of doing the lesson you prepared. Always meet the student's needs, regardless of your original plans.

When teaching a specific language skill, you can use the following lesson plan formats to introduce new material.

✦ Pronunciation

1. *Listen* to the student read a passage, and record it on audiotape.
2. *Identify* pronunciation problems, such as omission of final consonant sounds or the inability to pronounce /l/ and /r/ correctly.
3. Focusing on one problem sound at a time, *demonstrate* the correct tongue and mouth position.
4. *Model* the sound for the student, and have the student practice while looking in a mirror.
5. Ask the student to *practice* the sound in content reading. Underline each word with the sound the student is working on.
6. Ask the student to *monitor* his or her own speech to be sure of saying a specific sound correctly.

✦ Listening/Speaking

1. *Record* a conversation or interview with the student on audiotape.
2. *Identify* situations that are troublesome.
3. *Practice* by role-playing special situations, such as going to the bank, a store, or the post office.
4. Have the student *listen* to good models of speech on television or audiotape.

✦ Writing

1. *Demonstrate* what you are teaching (e.g., through a model sentence, paragraph, or essay).

2. *Label* the parts of the model (e.g., subject and verb, topic sentence and thesis, body and conclusion).

3. *Provide* a writing topic of interest.

4. Have the student *write* one part at a time.

5. *Evaluate* the writing sample.

6. Have the student *modify* the writing sample.

✦ Reading

1. *Select* a passage of interest.

2. *Read aloud*. You and the student can alternate.

3. *Check* for comprehension of main ideas.

4. *Discuss* difficult vocabulary. Have the student try to guess the meanings of words from the context before looking in the dictionary. Organize nouns into the categories of person, place, and thing. Organize verbs by the type of action, such as eating (e.g., *nibble, sip, gobble*) or walking (e.g., *amble, shuffle, waddle*).

5. *Summarize* the main ideas.

✦ Grammar

1. *Teach* as problems arise in writing or speaking.

2. *Find* correct usage in reading samples.

3. *Practice* correct usage in writing and speaking. You may wish to use a good communicative grammar text with exercises that apply a certain grammar rule in a real-life situation, such as going to the grocery store.

Step 4: Summarize the Main Points of the Lesson

- Ask the student questions that review the main points of the lesson. If you are using a textbook, use an exercise at the end of the chapter.

- If the student has to remember a series of facts for an exam, help him or her create an acronym, such as the one in the title of this text.

- If it seems suitable, use a game to summarize and reinforce the lesson.

Step 5: Interview the Student

- At the end of the session, give the student an opportunity to ask questions about the class or explain what he or she would like to do in the next lesson.

- If you have used a new technique or activity, ask if the student liked it or if it was helpful.

Case Studies: Points of Interest

◆ Case Study 1

- Ms. Freeman uses a traditional classroom setup in which she stands in front of the students and the students sit at desks that face her.
- She reviews old material before beginning new material.
- The four students depend on the tutor to provide the materials and activities.

◆ Case Study 2

- Ms. Hawkins tutors Omar in her home office. They sit side-by-side.
- She interviews Omar and records information on the Student Information Card (see chapter 1).
- In this situation, the tutor depends on the student to provide most of the topics and materials.

◆ Case Study 3

- Although she must work in a traditional classroom, Ms. Rogers creates a feeling of partnership by sitting next to Kim Su.
- Ms. Rogers' first session takes the form of an interview, but in later sessions she follows the three middle steps of a lesson: review old material, introduce new material, and summarize new material before assigning homework.
- In this tutoring situation, the student relies on the tutor to provide the text and activities for improved pronunciation and speaking skills. The tutor relies on the student to practice new skills, complete assignments, and report problems outside class.

> All three tutors in the case studies illustrate how the tutoring format can be applied in part or as a whole according to the content and purpose of the session. Tutors need to be flexible and sensitive to students' needs. In all case studies the tutor and students form a partnership and share responsibilities. Progress depends on the students' involvement and willingness to communicate their needs to the tutor.

Observe and Reflect

Plan the classroom setup that you think would work best for you and your student. Consider the following:

- the location
- the seating arrangement
- access to proper lighting
- elimination of distractions (e.g., from noise, from other people)

Teacher Information Form

Name of teacher: _____

Name of student: _____

Name of parents: _____

Address: _____

Telephone: _____

Areas of English that require tutoring:
___ Grammar ___ Reading ___ Writing ___ Listening/Speaking

Content areas that require tutoring:
___ Math ___ Science ___ History ___ Other (Specify) _____

Title of textbook: _____

Publisher of textbook: _____

Teacher's summary of student's strengths and weaknesses in subject area:

Student's statement of specific topics to be addressed during tutoring sessions:

Unit 2: Assess

After you determine the student's goals, you will assess the student and determine realistic tutoring goals. Assessment of the students' language skills will help you choose appropriate activities, texts, and materials. This unit will show you how to assess skills with both tutor-generated and commercial tests, how to use the data from the assessment tool you have chosen to establish teaching objectives, and how to determine the personal, emotional, and cultural factors that may affect your student's ability to learn.

CHAPTER 4

"How do I know what to teach?"

Assess skills and determine students' goals.

An important first step for any tutor is to determine what the student needs to learn and how much the student already knows. You determine what to teach by knowing your student's purposes for learning English.

How do you get this information? Some should have been provided on the Student Information Card (see chapter 1). Besides that source, you may want to contact parents, a sponsoring agency, or an employer to determine what to teach. From these various sources, you may learn important information, for example, that a refugee student needs survival English, that the school-aged child benefits most from academic or content-based English, or that a professional desires English for job purposes. Depending on what the student needs, you may wish to focus on oral skills, literacy skills, or both.

You must also assess the students' language skill level. Skill levels range from beginning, to intermediate, to advanced, with finer distinctions noted by *high* or *low,* as in *high beginning.* You will need to know these distinctions (explained in this chapter) as you choose texts or materials.

Language assessment, that is, an evaluation of the student's abilities in listening, speaking, reading, and writing, gives you a starting point for planning lessons. An assessment tool is a means for you to gauge the student's level of language in oral skills (i.e., listening and speaking) and literacy skills (i.e., reading and writing). You need to know your student's language level in order to choose materials and methods appropriate to the student's ability and purposes.

> Some students arrive with little or no knowledge of English, others have had some background in English, however limited, and others are advanced in either oral or literacy skills or both. Your job is to determine how much background the student has and work from there.

Step 1: Assessing Oral Skills

First, determine how well your student understands and responds to oral English. A few ways to do this are listed below.

- *oral interviews:* The student responds to questions from the tutor.
- *oral response to picture cues:* The student describes people, places, things, or activities in a picture.
- *responses to radio or television broadcasts or video clips:* The student listens to or watches an audio or video clip and explains the main points.
- *retelling of stories:* The tutor reads or tells a story, and the student retells it.
- *role play:* The tutor asks the student to perform a role, such as responding to a salesperson, ordering in a restaurant, or telephoning for information.

Of the techniques listed, the oral interview is the quickest and easiest for determining your student's level. You could, however, use some of the methods listed above to assess progress in oral skills throughout the tutoring sessions.

✦ Oral Interview

The oral interview is the most common method of assessing oral proficiency. With this technique, you ask the student to provide personal information and express opinions. You begin with easy questions and proceed to more difficult questions, and use the results of the interview to evaluate the student's level.

You may want to talk to students beforehand to get them to relax and respond. Ask how they are doing, whether they are comfortable at the table, and how they like their school (or city, or job). Once an informal, comfortable atmosphere is established, begin the interview in the same informal manner. When interviewing students,

- Be relaxed and friendly, and repeat questions or statements if necessary.
- If you wish, explain a question or give examples to help a student get started and feel at ease.

- If you wish, record the interview on audiotape so you can refer to it later for specific grammar or pronunciation problems that you are not necessarily focusing on during the interview.

Stop the interview if the student
- does not respond to the initial discussion
- does not understand the questions
- answers in one or two words only or through gestures
- does not respond at all
- through shrugs or other body language, shows an inability to answer

Use the information you have already accumulated for the evaluation. You have a beginning-level student.

In an oral interview, you may determine the student's skill level in one of two ways.

Method 1

Ask the student questions and give points for each answer (see the Oral Interview Grid included as a reproducible form at the end of this chapter). The number of correct responses will place the student along a continuum from the beginning to the advanced level. Begin with the easier questions, and continue until the student is no longer able to respond or does not respond correctly. Mark points according to this guideline:

- 2 points for a correct and clear answer in English
- 1 point for a response that is too short, is incomplete, or exhibits pronunciation and grammatical weaknesses
- 0 points for no response

Method 2

Use holistic screening. In this method, you simply compare your student's abilities with those listed on a scale.

Here are some general guidelines for determining levels:
- *Beginning-level* students are unable to respond, respond with gestures or one or two words, or are incomprehensible.
- *Intermediate-level* students understand and answer with short answers. If they do not understand, they ask for clarification, respond with appropriate but limited responses, or make an attempt to answer in sentences rather than one- or two-word answers. You can understand most responses.

- *Advanced-level* students understand easily, respond quickly, provide additional information, use mostly correct word choices and idiomatic speech, and are usually comprehensible.

The Language Range Finder Checklist, included as a reproducible form at the end of this chapter, describes the skills of students at various levels in more detail. Once you interview the students, you should be able to compare their abilities with the descriptors in the checklist.

> You could use both a point system and a holistic system to score the oral interview. Doing so will give you a better result.

Step 2: Assessing Literacy Skills

You want to know how much your student can read and write, both in the native language and in English. Here are some tools you can use to find out.

✦ Technique for Determining Literacy in the First Language

To determine literacy skills in the first language (L1), simply have the students write a little about themselves or their family, in their native language. The fact that you may not be able to read what they write is not important. If the students refuse or hesitate, assume for the time being that they cannot write their native language. Students who write several sentences are comfortable writing and have some degree of literacy in the native language. Then ask the student to read the work to you, and check to see if the student reads effortlessly and fluently.

If your students are literate in their native language, you will use that knowledge in constructing your own lessons. Literacy skills transfer. Even for students who do not use the Roman alphabet, the skill of reading symbols on a page is one on which you can build. Literate students know what reading is; they just need the key to unlock the code.

If your students have already mastered the Roman alphabet, you will be able to introduce some writing activity into each lesson as an important tool to help the student improve language skills. For students who are not literate or for those who use a different alphabet, you will have to spend some time introducing letters and sounds as you work on oral skills (see Appendix A for texts and Internet sites that offer materials for teaching the alphabet).

✦ Techniques for Determining Literacy in English

Whether or not your students demonstrate conversational skills, they might have a background in reading English. The next step is to determine whether they can read and understand English passages. You will want to test two types of reading skills:

- reading aloud, to determine decoding skills (i.e., the ability to sound out words on a page)
- reading silently and responding to questions, oral or written, to test comprehension

You might have on hand three reading passages for use in such an assessment: one for low-level or beginning-level readers, one for intermediate-level readers, and one for more advanced-level readers. At the end of this chapter is a reproducible form containing three suggested reading passages, one at each level. If you do not wish to use these selections, choose your own from texts, from the Internet, or from materials at your local library or literacy council. You might select readings that are designed for different age groups and different levels. For young learners, choose appropriate reading passages from children's books.

Assessing Decoding Skills

To assess decoding skills, have the students read a passage in English aloud, and record the reading on audiotape if possible.

1. Choose a passage that matches your student's oral skill level. For example, if your student places at the low intermediate level for oral skills, have your student try to read the intermediate-level reading first. If that selection is too difficult, move to the beginning-level reading. If, on the other hand, the student reads the intermediate-level passage well and understands it easily, move on to the advanced-level selection.

2. As the student reads, or as you listen to the recording of the reading, mark or underline the words and phrases that seem to cause difficulty. Note particularly the sounds or sound-letter correspondences that cause the student difficulty.

Students sometimes read words that are not in the passage but that make sense. Good readers predict what they expect to see rather than what they see. A mistake resulting from this prediction (called a *miscue*) might actually be a sign of an experienced reader, and you will want to note it. For example, the student might see "Will wonders never happen?" but read "Will wonders never cease?" Also, note whether the student uses any strategies for reading unfamiliar words.

Assessing Comprehension

If a student can read a passage, you may want to know how well he or she understood it.

1. Give the student a few minutes to reread the passage silently.

2. Ask the student what the reading was about. You may discuss this with the student briefly before moving on to questions about the reading. Begin with *yes/no* questions and proceed to information questions (i.e., questions beginning with *who, when, where,* or *why*). Allow the student to skim or scan the passage for information. This will give you an idea of the student's ability to use reading strategies.

3. If the student can respond easily to your questions, continue by having the student retell the information or summarize the passage.

4. Compare your student's abilities to the descriptions in the General Guidelines for Literacy Skill Levels, included as a reproducible form at the end of this chapter. This will give you a general idea of the student's ability.

> You may allow the student, particularly an older adolescent or adult, to choose the reading material. To do this, have on hand a selection of various levels of reading, from a beginning-level reader with little text and lots of pictures to more demanding reading, and several types of reading matter, such as greeting cards, magazines, newspapers, children's books, and encyclopedias. Ask the student to select something to read. The texts the student chooses may be an indication of the reading level. By having students choose the material, you are allowing them to show you their level.

Step 3: Assessing Writing Skills

After you have a good idea of your students' speaking and reading level, you may wish to assess their writing level. Limit your writing assessment to those students you have determined to be at least at the low intermediate level because writing is often considered to be an advanced skill and depends on skills in structure, vocabulary use, and reading. With beginning-level students, you will use oral skills as a basis for building reading and writing skills; in other words, students will learn to read and write as an integrated activity related to what they learn orally. To determine whether they can write at all, you might have beginning-level students write their names and fill out a form, such as an application form, with their address and telephone number.

An easy writing assessment, of course, is one in which you ask students to write something. You might, however, frame the assessment more specifically. For example, you might ask the student to write a short letter asking for travel information or explaining the return of an item to a manufacturer. For low intermediate–level students, you may wish to structure the assessment even more by providing some of the text, such as a dialogue, letter, or story, and having the student fill in sentences or words that complete the text. You do not have to write a text yourself; choose a paragraph or two from one of the reading passages, and create blanks.

Language teachers have found that some topics elicit better writing samples than others. These topics, some of which are given below, have almost universal appeal:

- Write a note to an English-speaking friend advising that person on a famous place to visit in your country. Explain what it is and why it is so famous.

- Describe a place in the world you would like to visit, and tell why.

- Tell about your favorite foods and any foods from your country that you recommend that I try.

The Guidelines for Writing Skill Levels, a reproducible form at the end of this chapter, will help you decide the student's writing skill level. Knowing this will not only help you place the student in the correct level and choose texts but will also give you some guidelines for determining how much writing you can ask of the student in the tutoring sessions and in assignments. For a student at the beginning or low intermediate level, you will want to work on basic writing, from the formation of letters; to writing and spelling names, addresses, and other personal information; to filling out forms and composing short notes and letters. The student's goal will help you decide what types of writing activities are appropriate.

Other Means of Assessing

✦ Samples of Student Work

If you are working with a school-aged learner, you can ask the parents, teacher, or student for examples of the student's work. Once you see the writing samples or the quizzes and tests, you will have a better idea of what you need to work on in your sessions. You might wish to contact the teacher for information on the student's work in class. The Teacher Information Form shown in chapter 3 is one way of getting teachers' feedback on students' needs.

If you can work with the student's teacher, you can provide invaluable assistance in the content areas. The student will learn English as well as content, and the tutoring sessions will be practical and helpful. Students who see progress in school are motivated to continue learning. Remember that the teacher may have a better understanding of what the students need than they themselves do. Students are sometimes unable to diagnose their own problems, and the teacher's input is very helpful.

✦ Self-Assessment

Older students who are at the intermediate level or above may provide you with a self-assessment of their skills (see the reproducible Student Self-Assessment Checklist at the end of this chapter). Self-assessments are an indication of the students' evaluation of their own skills and of the areas where they feel a needs for work. The students may also indicate personal goals (see Student's Goals for Tutoring, a reproducible form at the end of this chapter). Self-assessment provides you with some valuable information.

✦ Formal Assessment

Two formal assessments of overall language ability are the dictation and the cloze test. Both are easy to administer and evaluate.

Dictation

Once you have determined that the student can write English, you can give a short dictation:

1. Choose a text that neither is too advanced nor includes technical words (see Figure 1 for a sample).

2. Ask the student to listen. Read through the entire passage at normal speed while the student listens.

3. Now begin reading the passage slowly, allowing the student to write as you dictate.

4. If you wish, read through the entire passage once more.

5. After the student has completed the dictation, review the written passage.

If you give a dictation, you can evaluate students' ability to listen, understand, and write English. The dictation will tell you whether the students are using invented spelling or making wrong sound-letter correspondences. If the students show few or no problems with writing from dictation, you can dictate information to them during your sessions with the confidence that they will be able to write down the information accurately. If you notice that a student has difficulty, you will have to monitor that student's writing during the sessions.

Cloze

With the cloze procedure, you choose a passage and delete words, leaving blanks. The student must read the passage and fill in the blanks with words that will help the passage make sense. Follow these steps:

1. Choose a passage of 100–150 words. Do not choose anything technical or difficult (see Figure 2 for a sample).

2. Leave the first and last sentences intact.

3. Delete every seventh word beginning with the second sentence (unless the word is a number or a proper name). Some of the blanks will require structure words (e.g., prepositions, articles, or intensifiers) whereas others will require content words (i.e., nouns, verbs, adjectives, or adverbs).

4. After the student has completed the cloze, review the answers.

Figure 1. Sample Dictation Passage

Would the world be different if everyone spoke the same language? The answer is probably not, but it would make things much easier. People always look for better ways to communicate. If they don't speak the same language, they rely on translators, both human and computer. People want to communicate directly though. That may be one of the reasons why so many people learn English. Because so many people around the world learn it and use it, English has become, in a way, everyone's second language. It really does not belong to any one country. It belongs to the world. (100 words)

Figure 2. Sample Cloze Passage (Adapted From Johnston, 2000)

The Road to Ipswich

A man is walking to the town of Ipswich. He comes to a fork in _(1)_ road, with the two branches leading _(2)_ two different directions. He knows that _(3)_ of them goes to Ipswich, but _(4)_ doesn't know which one. He also _(5)_ that in the house right beside _(6)_ fork in the road there are _(7)_ brothers, identical twins, both of whom _(8)_ the road to Ipswich. He knows one brother always lies and the _(9)_ always tells the truth, but he _(10)_ tell them apart. What single question can he ask to whoever answers his knock on the door which will indicate to him the correct road to Ipswich?

Answers:

1. the	6. the
2. in	7. two
3. one	8. know
4. he	9. other
5. knows	10. cannot

The cloze test reveals sensitivity to English structure and appropriate vocabulary use. Students who are unable to fill in a blank or who use words incorrectly show a lack of vocabulary or a lack of understanding of the structure and function of words. You can evaluate the cloze test by accepting any substitution that is appropriate and makes sense. If the student shows at least 70% accuracy, you can assume some ability in vocabulary and structure. If the student scores less than 70%, you will want to include some work on English structure or grammar in your tutoring sessions.

✦ Ongoing Assessment

Early assessment helps you determine the students' levels and needs. Ongoing assessment helps you monitor the students' needs throughout the tutoring.

You might, for example, note problems that were not apparent on the initial assessment but that you observe during tutoring. Make a note of those on the Student Information Card. The students themselves may indicate problems that you did not detect. Keep a record of activities that work well with the student as well as those that are not effective. You should also, of course, assess all skills throughout the sessions.

Case Studies: Points of Interest

✦ Case Study 1

- Before meeting the Somali women, Ms. Freeman learns from the sponsoring agency that the women have very low literacy skills in their L1 and that they do not know how to read or speak English.

- The Somali women have told the translator that they want to be able to shop, count, and explain illnesses to the doctor.
- Ms. Freeman is careful to assess each student individually after each lesson. She does this by taking careful notes on the strengths and weaknesses of each student.

✦ Case Study 2

- Ms. Hawkins interviews Omar in an informal way, talks to his parents about his needs, and indicates that she will call the teacher about his schoolwork and have the teacher complete the Teacher Information Form.
- She looks at Omar's schoolwork and has him complete a short writing exercise.
- She uses the audiotape recorder to document Omar's speaking ability during his first session.

✦ Case Study 3

- Kim Su and her husband have indicated a desire for her to develop better communication skills.
- Ms. Rogers spends the first session having her student respond orally on audiotape. She does not give a reading and writing assessment.
- Ms. Rogers determines that Kim Su is very advanced in English but has some specific pronunciation problems and possibly some cultural barriers that inhibit her from communicating effectively.
- Because Kim Su is an adult with good reading and writing skills, Ms. Rogers has her complete a self-assessment.

Observe and Reflect

1. Create a cloze test for your student by selecting a reading and using the guidelines in this chapter. Be sure to consider your student's age and language level.
2. Select a short passage you could use as a dictation for your student.
3. List three topics that you could ask your student to write about in order to show writing skills.
4. Find a reading that would be appropriate for testing your student's reading and pronunciation skills.

Oral Interview Grid

Level	Question	Points (0, 1, 2)
Beginning	What is your name?	
	Where do you live?	
	Where were you born?	
	What day is today?	
Intermediate	Do you go to school? Do you work?	
	What kind of (school)work do you do?	
	Tell me what you did last weekend.	
	What are your plans for tomorrow (next year, the future)?	
Advanced	What kind of books (movies, music) do you enjoy?	
	Why do you want to study English?	
	What do you like to do for fun when you are not working or studying?	
	Tell me something about your family.	
	Total points (of 24 possible)	

Scoring (See the Language Range Finder Checklist for descriptions of each level.)
Beginning   0–8 points
Intermediate   9–16 points
Advanced   17–24 points

Language Range Finder Checklist

Level	Description
Low beginning	The student • can barely answer the question, "What's your name?" • cannot give you an address and telephone number • does not understand most of your questions • cannot tell you about himself or herself or about his or her family • contacts you through an interpreter who says the student knows very little English • cannot read or fill out the Student Information Card
High beginning	The student • can answer most questions on the Student Information Card but makes spelling errors • can answer one-word response questions but has trouble with questions about problems and goals that require the use of phrases and sentences • understands your questions if you speak very slowly and use simple sentences, and frequently asks you to repeat • answers your questions in one-word responses or short phrases, never in complete sentences • often mispronounces words and makes many grammar mistakes • needs to be prompted frequently for repetition because mistakes prevent you from understanding
Low intermediate	The student • can write answers to all the questions on the Student Information Card • understands you when you speak at a normal speed but occasionally asks you to repeat • speaks in complete sentences but loses control of grammar in long, complex sentences • uses a few pronunciations that make speech incomprehensible but is understandable most of the time
High intermediate	The student • speaks of a need for help with reading and of having to use a dictionary frequently • writes in complete sentences with few errors when describing problems and goals on the Student Information Card • understands your questions about life in his or her native country when you speak at normal speed • pronounces clearly but makes some mistakes with idioms and grammar
Low advanced	The student • can describe needs clearly • makes no spelling or grammar errors on the Student Information Card and gives very complete information about problems and goals • never asks you to repeat anything you say when you speak at a normal speed • occasionally has to search for the right word or misuses an idiom or grammar structure

Passages for Assessing Reading Skill
(Adapted from Johnston, 2000)

Laws and People

Every country has laws to help its people. The laws allow people to live together without too many disagreements. People accept the laws to help settle arguments and avoid fights. People who don't accept the laws cause problems and even civil war.

There are special places where judges and juries decide laws. These places are called courts. Everyone must agree to accept the ruling of the courts or the court system will not work. In democratic countries, for example, people agree to accept laws about elections. The winner is the new leader. In a trial, all the people involved agree to accept the ruling of the court even if they don't agree with it. They accept the law of the court. As long as they accept their country's laws, people will have peace. (133 words)

Sample Questions
- Do laws help people live together peacefully?
- Does every country have laws for its people?
- Who decides on laws?
- Where do judges and juries decide on laws?
- Must everyone agree on the court's ruling?

Intermediate–High Intermediate Level

Resolving Arguments in Society

Society creates ways of helping its members resolve arguments. If ways did not exist, it might be impossible for people to agree on various issues, such as who rules the country or even where to place a fence between neighbors' houses. Without citizens agreeing on ways of resolving arguments, there might be civil strife or even civil war.

Special places exist to settle arguments. States and towns have courts to settle disputes between people. In order for the court system to work, though, everyone must agree to accept its results.

In democratic countries, for example, the people have agreed to accept the process that declares the winner in an election, and that winner is the leader of all the people. In a court trial, all people involved agree to accept the verdict of the jury. Society remains at peace as long as everyone agrees to accept the processes and the results of the procedures designed to handle disputes and arguments. (160 words)

- Can civil strife occur if people do not agree on ways of settling arguments?
- Must people accept the results of the court system?
- Who decides the winner in a dispute in court?
- What is a verdict?
- Why do people accept verdicts they don't like?

Advanced

Resolving Arguments in Society

It is, of course, essential for any continuing peaceful order in society and in one's personal life that agreed-upon methods for resolving arguments be in place. Without them, certain decisions might be impossible to make with any hope of securing agreement, and at times the argument may degenerate into active hostility and physical violence (resolving the dispute by brute force, without any rules). The latter is generally a sign that whatever is supposed to be working to resolve disagreements is no longer effective. And when such violence takes over an entire society, its culture has broken down in the most serious way possible (i.e., in civil war).

For that reason, we insist that judicial arguments, legislative debates, industrial disputes, divorce mediation, and so on take place in specially designated places and according to agreed upon processes and rules, rather than in the back streets. And for the same reason we agree to abide by the processes we have set up to resolve the argument, even if the result is not always what we had hoped for.

Thus, for example, in a democratic country the people agree that the winner in an election will be the leader of all the people and that the verdict of the jury will decide the matter once and for all in a murder trial. In any situation where we begin to abandon our agreement that such decisions will resolve the issue (e.g., by taking the law into our own hands if the result does not satisfy us), the fabric of society starts to experience important and dangerous tensions. (264 words)

Sample Questions

- What keeps society from breaking down because of disagreements or disputes?
- Must the resolution of disagreement take place in special places?
- What does using brute force show about a society?
- What do people agree to when someone wins an election?
- Why might society begin to "experience important and dangerous tensions"?

Adapted from *Essays and Arguments, Section Two,* by I. Johnston, 2000, http://www.mala.bc.ca /~johnstoi/arguments/argument2.htm. Copyright released May 2000.

General Guidelines for Literacy Skill Levels

Level	Description
Beginning	The student • probably is illiterate or demonstrates low literacy in the native language • may speak a language that does not use the Roman alphabet, such as those used in countries in Asia and the Middle East and those using the Cyrillic alphabet This student will learn the alphabet and begin copying words learned in the new alphabet.
Intermediate	The student • shows an ability to recognize letters and sounds • can pronounce some words accurately but skips over or mispronounces other words • demonstrates some knowledge of what he or she has read This student can benefit from working on materials that will help improve vocabulary, introduce new structures, and challenge the student intellectually.
Advanced	The student • demonstrates mastery of the readings, that is, can read and comprehend with little problem • often comes to tutoring because oral skills are weaker than reading skills or because specialized English study is required

Guidelines for Writing Skill Levels

Level	Description
Low beginning	The student • does not write anything in English, or may write his or her name only • may know some letter names and write some words if they are spelled out • can begin copying words
High beginning	The student • may write a few words and can write a word if it is spelled out • may begin writing simple sentences • may be able to write words he or she can say, but spelling may not always be accurate
Low intermediate	The student • can write short letters and respond to questions in writing • may require some help with spelling but can develop dictionary skills • can perform guided writing activities
High intermediate	The student • can express himself or herself by writing short paragraphs and essays • can write descriptions and narrations and respond to questions in a textbook • can perform most social functions of writing (notes, letters, invitations) • can develop academic writing skills (e.g., writing essays and reports)
Low advanced	The student • can write for different audiences and knows the difference between formal and informal writing • may still need work on writing conventions, such as punctuation • except for some problems with idioms, writes with near-nativelike ability • may need some work on acceptable rhetorical styles in English writing

Student Self-assessment Checklist

Name: _____ Date: _____

Check (✔) the box that shows your skills in English.

Skill	Not very well	A little	Fairly well	Well	Comments
I can speak English					
I can read English					
I can write English					
I can understand when someone speaks to me at work or at school					
I can talk on the telephone					
I can use English to take care of my needs					

Student's Goals for Tutoring

Mark the boxes for the skills you want to improve. Use * for the most important and ✔ for the least important. For each skill, tell what you can do now and what you want to be able to do.

Skill		Now I can . . .	I want to be able to . . .
Speaking			
Listening			
Reading			
Writing			
Pronunciation			

CHAPTER 5

"How do I use assessment to help me teach?"

Use assessment to determine tutoring goals and establish a starting point.

You have now completed an assessment and have an idea of the students' needs and abilities. You have probably found that your students, unless they are absolute beginners, already have some knowledge of English. Use that knowledge as the starting point, and apply it to other situations, activities, or knowledge. In other words, start with what they have (see Table 1 for suggestions).

Students might say they want to "begin with chapter 1" because they feel insecure about their knowledge of and ability in English. You can certainly do some review, but you do not need to reteach what the students already know; instead, reinforce it. One way of showing students what they know is to keep a checklist of what they can express (see chapter 10). Share this checklist with the students at each lesson. They will see progress, particularly as you add more information to it.

Before you begin making lesson plans, you need an overall plan of what you are going to teach, how you will teach it, and what goals you want to reach. In academic settings, you would call this a curriculum. For tutoring purposes, you may want to think of it as a roadmap to your student's language goals. Your overall plan can be as simple as a chart of general goals, such as the ones in the Case Studies: Points of Interest section in this chapter.

Table 1. Start With What They Have: Suggestions

If . . .	Extend that knowledge . . .
. . . your students can answer personal about other people's names, addresses, and profession,	. . . by having the students answer questions questions about their name, address, and professions.
. . . the students know and can recognize numbers,	. . . by having the students do simple arithmetic while learning terms such as *addition, multiplication,* and *fraction.*
. . . the students know even one or two things about an academic subject, such as history,	. . . by providing vocabulary and phrases as you help the student with that subject.
. . . the students know some generic terms, such as *fruit, vegetables,* or *meat,*	. . . by teaching them specific words, such as *apple, spinach,* or *beef.*

(See Tutor's Notes on Goals for Student, included at the end of the chapter as a reproducible form.)

> At first, having to decide what to teach will seem overwhelming. Your assessment, however, should have given you an idea of the student's most important needs. Limit your goals to working on those needs. If, for example, you have a beginning-level adult student who is trying to get a job and provide for a family, design a course of study that helps this student learn to communicate basic needs. Meeting this need—for what is sometimes referred to as *survival skills*—is an immediate goal.

Decide on a time frame even if the student has not stated how long the tutoring should last, then structure your lessons to fit your time frame. Then decide which skills the students need most and begin with those. The time frame helps you see success in increments. You may decide, for example, on a 6-week plan, a 2-month tutoring schedule, or semester-long tutoring. As you reach the end of the time frame, reassess the student to determine if the goals have been reached. Be conservative in your estimation, however, so that you avoid discouraging students. It is better to see them progress faster than you expected than to realize that they will not meet the goals you have set. You can always rework your curriculum if the students are making progress more quickly than you anticipated. They will just think you are a very gifted tutor who has helped them reach their goals quickly.

Also, if you set a time frame for completing the work, the students may not be too discouraged if they do not see results immediately. For example, if the students have received tutoring for 3 weeks and see no progress, but you have indicated that you will need 6 weeks to reach your goal, the 3-week difference may actually reassure the students. If it does not, you and they will know that expecting to reach your goals within the time frame is unrealistic. To make your lessons fit your time frame, choose the most important goals and begin by addressing them.

Goal Setting

✦ Example 1: Survival Skills for Beginning-Level Students

Generally, in teaching survival skills to beginning-level students, start by helping them learn to communicate personal information, such as their name, address, and telephone number. The students might also need to indicate age, marital status, and jobs formerly held. They should also begin using polite forms in English, such as *please* and *thank you.* After developing a personal language skill, the students might need to talk about such topics as family, health, transportation, food, clothing, housing, and occupations. You, perhaps with the help of the students' sponsor if there is one, can decide on the order of the topics to cover.

Then you must decide whether to focus entirely on spoken English or to include reading and writing. If the students are already literate, you will want to introduce some reading and writing activities appropriate to the topics you cover. Being able to fill out application forms for a driver's license or a job, for example, is a part of survival skills. If the students are not literate, you can encourage literacy by helping them recognize and write words they already know. Help them read *environmental print*, which is writing that is often seen in public places (e.g., store names and public signs). As you design your lessons, you may want to consult relevant books on teaching survival skills (see Appendix A). You might decide that you can accomplish your goals within a 2-month period if you meet with the students every day for 1½ hours. With a time frame in mind, you are ready to plan lessons and anticipate how many lessons in the book you can cover.

✦ Example 2: Academic English for Intermediate-Level Students

Intermediate-level students may need to work on improving all skills but may wish to concentrate on those that support their ultimate goals. If your student is a high school or college student, for example, your goals may be to help the student succeed in academic subjects.

Consult with the student's teachers, if possible, and work with them in supporting and guiding the student. You might set your time frame to correspond with the academic calendar. You might also choose to focus on one academic subject, such as social studies or English. Some schools issue progress reports after the first 6 or 8 weeks of a term. Reevaluate the student's success after the first progress report is issued. Together, you and the student will determine whether the goals have been met. If not, you may have to reassess the goals together.

The advanced-level student has a variety of special needs. Teaching or tutoring English for a special purpose is called English for specific purposes (ESP). For example, some students need to pass examinations in order to enter undergraduate or graduate college or university programs. In that case, work on academic reading and writing, with emphasis on vocabulary and reading comprehension. Some students may want to be able to communicate better with English-speaking colleagues in the workplace, in which case the goals of the tutoring have been defined for you—better communicative skills on a variety of topics, including work-related ones. Some advanced-level students need help with the language of their professional field. You may, for example, be asked to help with the English of health care, the legal system, or business. Some texts are especially designed for ESP, and a review of publishers' materials will help here (see Appendix A; consider particularly University of Michigan Press's ESP publications). Once you have decided on the area to cover and the material to use, you and the student can decide on the time frame.

> To give the student something to anticipate and work toward, use a date as a deadline for meeting a goal, such as the date of a standardized exam, an office party, or a presentation at work.

What About Grammar?

Notice that we have not yet used the word *grammar*. Unless you are working with a student who needs to pass a standardized test or who is writing academic papers, you probably will not teach grammar as a subject. Think of grammar as a tool. With students who know grammatical terminology (e.g., *noun, verb, phrases, active voice, clause*), you can use it to help them focus on their learning and correct their errors. For many of your students, however, your design for the lessons will be more a reflection of each student's individual needs than a review of a grammar text.

Your own language learning experiences can help or hinder you as you tutor. If you have studied a foreign language, you might choose to tutor using the method with which you are most familiar. Your experiences, however, were probably in a classroom with other literate students learning a foreign language, and you probably did not need to communicate with native speakers. Your ESL students, by contrast, are learning a second language. They will have many opportunities to hear English spoken and see it written, and they may need to communicate in it almost immediately. (They cannot wait a year to learn past tense, for example, as you may have done in foreign language class.) You, on the other hand, may not speak your students' native language and will have to use English to teach English. Therefore, your students will learn grammar inductively (i.e., inferring rules from the information presented) at the beginning level but may benefit from deductive learning (i.e., applying rules learned to new environments) at the intermediate to the advanced level. You are in charge of the learning and are not bound by the order of information as it is presented in texts or standardized syllabi. Remember that you are tutoring because your student needs individual help, including an individualized plan and goals.

If you do not teach grammar as a subject, then what do you teach? Think of language as more than just grammar and vocabulary. People use language to communicate, and within this broad function you can approach the language to be learned in various ways (see Table 2) and design your lessons accordingly. Experienced teachers organize language into teachable chunks and focus on one or more aspects appropriate to the student and the situation. You might even combine some of the approaches shown in Table 2. For example, you might teach the language of a specific function (e.g., offering aid or help in a health care situation) and then teach the grammar forms used for the function (in this case, modal auxiliaries, as in *"May* I help?" and *"Would* you like some help?").

Our point here is simple. In a tutoring environment, you, the tutor, are the ultimate authority on which aspects of language to teach and in which order to teach them. A textbook or prepared syllabus is only a tool to help you reach your goals. You decide what to teach based on an assessment of the student and the information you get about the student's immediate needs. You and the student together determine the goals for the tutoring.

Table 2. Different Approaches to Language Study

Approach	Explanation
Grammar	Students focus on the structure of language and manipulate the various components (i.e., parts of speech) in oral or written exercises. This traditional approach to teaching foreign language is appropriate for meeting some but not all students' needs.
Situations	Students practice the language and vocabulary of specific situations they will encounter, such as being at the bank, at the mall, or in a restaurant.
Topics	The lessons are organized around themes, such as *health food* or *clothing*. The survival skills approach relies heavily on this approach.
Functions	Students focus on what they need to do with language, such as give a report, make a speech, describe items, identify things, or seek information.
Skills	Students work on developing a specific skill, such as listening to lectures, talking on the telephone, or writing letters or memos.
Tasks	Students learn language through problem-solving activities in which they must follow directions, complete a puzzle, or follow written or oral instructions.

Case Studies: Points of Interest

✦ Case Study 1

- Ms. Freeman, with the help of a bilingual interpreter, determines that the Somali women are at the beginning or high beginning level. They have immediate needs related to their families: They want to be able to shop, perform simple math calculations related to money, and explain illnesses to the doctor (see Figure 1 for Ms. Freeman's notes on Halima).

- She plans to conduct tutoring for 1–1½ hours each day for 8 weeks in a very intensive program.

- She decides to build on the students' experiences. The students understand the use of money and want to learn how to count in English. They are responsible for the health of their families and want to explain health problems to doctors and other medical personnel. They are interested in knowing the names of body parts so they can describe aches and pains. They all know how to cook, so Ms. Freeman plans to cover shopping and cooking terms.

✦ Case Study 2

- Ms. Hawkins determines through her assessment of Omar, her conversation with his parents, and ultimately her conversation with his teachers that Omar needs help and support in his academic subjects, particularly those that require much reading and writing, such as social studies (see Figure 2 for Ms. Hawkins' goals for Omar).

- She notes that Omar likes the personal attention of a tutor and may learn better in a tutoring environment than in the classroom.

- Although she diagnoses weak pronunciation, she will focus on reading and writing, working on pronunciation only when it interferes with Omar's ability to write and spell accurately.

- She will communicate with Omar's teachers to find out what work he has in school.

Figure 1. Tutor's Notes for Case Study 1

Tutor: *Ms. Freeman*				
Student's name	What to teach	How to teach	Goals to meet	How long to teach
Halima	Survival English	Hands-on; games; real-world activities	She should be able to take care of some basic personal needs. She and I will decide which ones.	Every day for 8 weeks; 1 to 1½ hours a day

Figure 2. Tutor's Notes for Case Study 2

Tutor: *Ms. Hawkins*				
Student's name	What to teach	How to teach	Goals to meet	How long to teach
Omar	Academic subjects and appropriate English	Focus on reading and writing relating to school subjects	He should begin understanding school subjects and improving grades. We have agreed that his goal is to make at least a grade of "C" on his work.	Twice a week for a semester; 2 hours each session.

✦ Case Study 3

- Ms. Rogers determines that the goal of improving pronunciation and conversational ability will help Kim Su whether she continues to work in nursing (her goal) or use English in social settings (her husband's goal) (see Figure 3 for Ms. Rogers' notes).

- Ms. Rogers chooses a text (*Well Said*; Grant, 2001) to help with the tutoring because it is designed specifically for students like Kim Su. It allows the student to be self-directed and do much self-assessment.

- On a scale of 1–6, Kim Su rates herself as a 2 but says she wants to be a 4. This assessment gives Ms. Rogers a specific goal for the tutoring.

- Ms. Rogers can individualize the sessions for this student because of information she has about the predictable problems of Chinese speakers (from *Learner English*; Swan & Smith, 2001). She will focus on those problems in the sessions.

Figure 3. Tutor's Notes for Case Study 3

Tutor: *Ms. Rogers*				
Student's name	What to teach	How to teach	Goals to meet	How long to teach
Kim Su	Pronounciation and communication skills	Use a text and follow closely; allow self-assessment	She should be able to carry on a conversation in an informal social situation. We will plan a small party at the end of the tutoring to test the results.	Twice a week for 3 months; 1 hour each session

Observe and Reflect

1. Check Web sites for materials that might be suitable for your student's level.
2. Make your own chart with information you deem important, or copy the reproducible form.

Tutor's Notes on Goals for Student

Tutor:				
Student's name	What to teach	How to teach	Goals to meet	How long to teach

CHAPTER 6

"What factors can help or hinder a student's English learning ability?"

Consider personal, cultural, and linguistic factors.

Despite well-designed lessons and an eager and knowledgeable tutor, students sometimes fail. On the other hand, working with few or no materials and an untrained volunteer tutor, some students make great strides. What accounts for this?

Actually, many factors add up to predict success for a particular learner, and not all of them are known. You will want to be aware of some factors, however, in order to adapt the tutoring sessions to accommodate them. Here we consider three types of factors: personal, cultural, and linguistic.

What Are Personal Factors?

Language teachers often remark that some students seem to be natural language learners. They pick up a language effortlessly and begin speaking a new language very quickly. Do such students really exist? If so, what abilities do these students have? Four personal factors contribute to—or hinder—success in language learning: degree of extroversion or introversion, preferred learning style, motivation, and age. Once you find out your student's personal factors, you can adjust your approach accordingly.

✦ Extroversion

Students who are extroverted are very outgoing and use their newly acquired language features whenever possible. Extroverted students are willing to use the language despite the possibility of making mistakes. They learn well through interaction with others, forcing others to provide language input. On closer observation, students who seem to use language effortlessly actually make quite a few errors, but their willingness to keep talking and their outgoing nature helps listeners understand the message.

The Challenge

You face a challenge in tutoring the extrovert. For one thing, the student needs personal interaction, but you may be the only available native-English-speaking conversation partner. Even if you structure the sessions to provide as many opportunities as possible for the student to engage in conversation, the student may not want to take the time to monitor output for accuracy or to spend much time mastering the fine points of grammar.

What Can You Do?

Use the student's natural gregariousness to support language learning. You might consider assigning activities outside the tutoring session in which the student must seek information from others, such as administering questionnaires or conducting interviews that become reports for you. You can also provide the student with opportunities for speaking and writing within and outside the sessions, such as having the student write e-mail messages to you or send you notes.

Wanting to use the language and converse with others can be a positive trait that you will want to encourage. However, extroverts can sometimes become so involved in wanting to use language that they neglect the difficult task of analyzing and making sense of language through reflection and study. Accurate use of language is an area on which you will have the extrovert focus. You will need to develop means of drawing the student's attention to accuracy, such as modeling correct forms, cueing, or overt correction.

✦ Introversion

Introversion is the personal characteristic that makes some people more likely to find fulfillment within themselves rather than through interaction with others. Students who are introverts, for example, might prefer analyzing the language over using it with others, particularly when they are unsure of their own skills. Such students feel comfortable speaking with the tutor in one-to-one sessions but are less willing to speak to other native speakers or to people they do not know well.

The Challenge

Students who are introverted may be reluctant to speak but may spend time on reading, writing, and language exercises. They may not take an active part in large classes or may be overshadowed by the extroverted student.

What Can You Do?

Students who are introverted need encouragement to communicate with others. They benefit from taking part in structured activities using language they have mastered. You can help by providing this encouragement through activities such as role plays, in which students rehearse language.

Value what this student can do, and build from there. Your introverted student, for example, may perform well in writing activities and display more accuracy in language use when conversing. In that case, you and the student can create dialogues for situations the student encounters and practice them together.

✦ Learning Styles

The Challenge

Different students use different strategies to learn.
- Some are *visual learners,* who write down what they learn or prefer seeing it written.
- Some are *auditory learners,* who remember what they hear and may want you to explain something rather than read about it themselves.
- Some are *kinesthetic learners,* who learn best by doing, or experiencing their environment through their senses. They like to become involved in activities that require the use of language.

What Can You Do?

As you work with students, you develop a better understanding of the kinds of activities the students enjoy and the ones in which they find success. The students, especially older ones, should be able to tell you the activities they like and those that work for them.

Adapt your activities to your particular learner in each session. Especially for young children, kinesthetic learning in the form of play is an important language learning activity and should be integrated into the sessions. Older children, too, benefit from hands-on activities, including drawing, designing, making choices, and becoming involved physically in whatever they are learning. Use a combination of listening, reading, and writing activities whenever you can.

✦ Motivation

Motivation is one of the most important predictors of success in learning a foreign language. Whether students need English for success at school, for job advancement, or for personal reasons, motivated students show larger gains in language learning than unmotivated students do. Those who want to integrate into the community with the ultimate goal of becoming U.S. citizens have much invested in learning English. Those who see that learning English benefits them personally will spend time, money, and effort on classes and tutoring sessions. Such students are often a joy to work with.

The Challenge

Students who are receiving tutoring under duress may not be so motivated. They may come to you because their parents have forced them to come to improve language skills. Their teachers may have recommended tutoring because of poor grades. Some adults may come because they feel pressured to learn English, but the responsibilities of family and job make them too tired to spend much time on it, so they become discouraged.

What Can You Do?

Knowing a little about your students' background will help you understand the various challenges they face. Sometimes giving the students short-term goals to reach and helping them reach those goals will inspire them to continue.

✦ Age

The learner's age is another factor to consider. Young learners will eventually acquire a second language (L2), given enough time and opportunity, and, depending on their age, may even become bilingual and sound like native speakers. This ability to acquire native speaker pronunciation becomes more difficult as people age.

The older learner has strengths, too. Learners in their teens or 20s, especially those who are already literate in their first language (L1), can use their literacy skills to support their learning of an L2 and may become quite proficient. Adults can use their knowledge and experience of the world as tools to help them learn and, given the opportunity, can actually acquire a language more rapidly than a very young child can.

The Challenge

Some learners, particularly those who are middle aged or older, find learning an L2 some-what of a challenge, especially if they have never done so before. (There is some evidence that the more languages a person learns, the easier it is to learn new ones.) For you, this means that the older learner presents special challenges.

Adult learners, too, have many responsibilities and may not be able to devote as much time to learning and using a new language as young learners can. Children, for example, learn and use English to a certain extent by playing with English-speaking children; older learners might not have the opportunity to be around native English speakers. Progress for older learners who cannot devote much time to language learning may be slow, and they may face frustration in the effort.

What Can You Do?

The younger the learner, the more you will want to vary the activities within each session. In addition, find materials suitable to the learner's age group. We do not recommend using children's books with adults—under any circumstances—just because the reading level is low. Instead, use high interest, low-level reading materials available for ESL or emerging literacy students.

Knowing that adults do not like to appear foolish when they make mistakes, you can make the sessions relaxed and interesting. With adult learners, humor goes a long way. A relaxed session in which mistakes are allowed and students and tutor feel comfortable laughing at themselves will ease the students' tension and frustration over trying to express themselves using simple, unsophisticated language. In addition, remember that older learners need to participate in what and how they learn. They often know what they want to learn and how they best learn. You will need to exercise patience and use as many strategies as you can to support the older learner.

In coping with personal factors, your role is to be aware of the signals learners send and adapt and adjust as necessary. You do not need to go by the book. One of the advantages of one-on-one tutoring is that you can adapt the sessions for your student's age and preferred learning style.

What Are Some Cultural Factors?

✦ Acculturation

Acculturation is the process of adapting to a new culture. Students who come from cultures similar to U.S. culture, that is, from Western and industrialized societies, might adapt more quickly to living in the United States than students whose cultures differ radically. Nevertheless, most new arrivals and even people who have been in the United States for a time go through stages of cultural adjustment.

The Challenge

Acculturation has four basic stages:
1. At first, immigrants or visitors are happy and euphoric to be in the new country. Everything seems exciting and interesting.
2. As life becomes more difficult, language problems persist, and nothing seems to work out, people begin to feel frustration, even hostility. In this stage, known as *culture shock*, newcomers may experience a dislike of the people and the culture of the new country

along with anger, unhappiness, sadness, homesickness, and even illness. During this time, students experience emotions that work against their acquiring English.

3. If they can work through the culture shock stage, immigrants or visitors may find that eventually problems get resolved, and they begin to accept, if not understand, the differences between the new culture and their own. They see that they are making progress. They get used to the customs and the country and might even begin to laugh off the inconveniences that arise.

4. Finally, the newcomers recover and begin to feel more comfortable in the new surroundings. At this stage, some individuals even act as guides and helpers to other new arrivals from their country. When this happens, the person has acculturated.

What Can You Do?

Be aware of the stages of acculturation. Sometimes, when a student demonstrates difficulty learning a language, it is the result of culture shock. Working through the culture shock may be more important than learning a language at the moment. You can use the language sessions to have students discuss their concerns.

✦ Surface and Deep Culture

After having acculturated, students often maintain many of their own cultural practices even though they intend to settle permanently in the United States. You may not always be aware of many of these practices, which include certain guidelines—even taboos—concerning, for example, women's dress, public behavior, and relationship of teacher and student.

Cultural factors that are overt are easier to understand and perceive. For example, many people know that Hindi women may wear saris and expect Japanese students to remove their shoes at the door of the house. Tutors may accept small gifts because many students feel it is important to honor teachers with tokens. Food, music, and dress are some of the cultural differences that interest tutors and provide some stimulating topics of discussion in the tutoring sessions. They are, however, only signs of *surface culture.*

The Challenge

Deep culture includes features that are not always visible—for example, how students feel about U.S. culture, what their notions of time and keeping appointments are, and what they consider to be topics of importance for their role in their society. You might eventually become frustrated, for example, if your students repeatedly tell you they understand an explanation and then immediately demonstrate a complete lack of understanding. You may tire of the students' constantly begging your forgiveness for being "an ignorant student" and then showing that they have actually mastered the material quite well. Some students might even tell you something that is not true—not because they want to lie but because for them telling you what you want to hear is more important. Understanding someone's deep cultural values is very difficult, and even with some explanation, you may find certain notions hard to accept.

Definitely allow students to share and explain cultural practices. Students are proud of their culture, and they will need to explain their cultural practices to others, too.

If a student displays behavior you find unusual or problematic, you may not know if it is the result of personal or cultural factors. For example, if you are being compensated for tutoring, you may have reminded the student several times about payment for the sessions, only to have the student ignore your request. You may not know if the issue of money is culturally taboo or if the student just refuses to pay. Or, when you ask a student to read an essay or story, the student may ignore your request or read something else. Was the subject of the essay or story embarrassing for the student, or did the student fail to understand your assignment? If such behavior persists, you may have to contact someone from the same culture or refer to a book on culture to determine the cause of the student's actions.

What Are Some Linguistic Factors?

✦ Language Interference

The Challenge

You may want to know something about the features of the students' native languages. Areas in which the languages differ from English, such as sounds, grammar, or word order, may be areas of *interference*, in which the students apply what they know from their native language to English.

For example, if the student's first language requires modifiers to follow the nouns they modify, as in Spanish or French, rather than precede them, as in English, students may use such phrases as *paper toilet* instead of *toilet paper*. If a sound exists in English but not in the native language, the learner will substitute a similar sound that exists in the native language. A French speaker may therefore say *zey* instead of *they*, or a Japanese student may say *lice* instead of *rice*. If a student's language does not use articles (i.e., *a, an,* and *the*), the student will have difficulty understanding and using them properly in English. For example, your Chinese student might write, "I need book."

What Can You Do?

Experienced ESL teachers know the types of errors to expect from learners they have worked with. You will develop that skill, too, as you work with students from the same language groups. You can also consult books, such as *Learner English* (Swan & Smith, 2001), or contact organizations, such as the Center for Applied Linguistics (see Appendix D), that provide information about various languages. Fortunately, much information is available over the Internet to help you understand features of your student's language.

Once you know what to anticipate, you can use that information to help plan your lessons. You can focus on those areas that cause problems and spend less time on those that pose no particular problems. It will also help you realize that some features will be particularly challenging for the student and may take much practice to master.

> Not all errors are the result of interference. Errors may also occur when students apply rules from English incorrectly to new structures. For example, the student who writes or says *eated* has applied a rule for past tense that resulted in an error (i.e., the *-ed* ending works for regular but not irregular verbs). This error results from overgeneralization. After students learn rules, they also eventually have to learn the exceptions. Remember that overgeneralization of rules is a natural part of the language acquisition process. As students begin to apply rules, help them learn the exceptions.

✦ Learner Speech

The Challenge

Another feature of language acquisition is the fascinating phenomenon of learner speech. Learners go through stages of acquiring language and do not immediately master the features you have taught so diligently. For example, learners have been shown to go through several stages in acquiring the negative in English, starting with using *no* as a negative marker (e.g., *I no want that*) to eventually using the correct marker (e.g., *I do not want that* or *I am not from the United States*). These are known as features of an *interlanguage*. Four stages of interlanguage have been described:

1. In the random error stage, the learner is not yet aware of the system of language.
2. In the emergent stage, the learner begins showing some consistency in language use and attempts to apply rules, although not always accurately.
3. The learner then begins to show more consistency and even to self-correct.
4. Finally, the learner has more or less mastered the system so that meaning is not obscured and there are relatively few errors.

What Can You Do?

Knowing the stages will help you discover where your students are in the acquisition process. Develop lessons that provide as much input as possible to the students so that they will see the systematic patterns of English. You will need to explain some forms explicitly to the students, particularly if they continue using inaccurate forms.

✦ Fossilized Speech

The speech of a student who plateaus at some point and ceases to acquire correct forms is said to have fossilized. An example is nonnative speakers of English who have been in the United States many years but who still maintain strong foreign accents and who continue to make errors in language use.

The Challenge

Because language has become a habit for these people, getting rid of fossilized forms and moving toward correct language requires much work.

What Can You Do?

Based on an accurate assessment of the student, list the areas of greatest concern, point them out to the student, and plan lessons around them. Keep a careful checklist of the items, and note the student's use. There will be some correction and then some backsliding, but with continued work the student should begin to show progress.

You should also develop ways of signaling to students that they have used an incorrect form while conversing. One tutor, for example, told a student that each time he used the incorrect form *you was* for *you were,* she would pull her earlobe as a signal. This signal became a visual cue to the student, and he began to monitor himself and self-correct.

✦ Cognates

Students are often surprised to see many words in English that they already recognize. What they are noting are the large number of cognates, that is, words from the L1 that are also found in the L2, possibly as a result of borrowing. English has borrowed heavily over the centuries and uses many words from other languages. The words shown in Table 1 are a small sample of the cognates English shares with other languages. As students discover these cognates, they may wish to let you know that their language has these words, too. Learning English seems easier to students as they realize they already know some vocabulary.

> Be aware of *false cognates*—words that look similar in two languages but have different meanings. Students may use a word that looks similar to one in their language only to find out that it means something quite different in English.

Table 1. Cognates in English

Source	Cognates
Arabic	alcohol, algebra, candy, coffee, cotton, giraffe, magazine, mattress, sofa, zero
Dutch	boss, caboose, coleslaw, cookie, cruise, golf, groove, landscape, spool, snoop, waffle
French	bayou, bureau, butte, cache, chowder, depot, gopher, levee, prairie
German	cobalt, hoodlum, kindergarten, loafer, lobby, noodle, ouch, poker, poodle, pretzel, protein, quartz, semester, seminar, waltz, zinc
Italian	balcony, balloon, bankrupt, cartoon, lasagne, pasta, piano, spaghetti, umbrella
Japanese	geisha, haiku, judo, karate, kimono, sake, tycoon
Slavic languages	intelligentsia, mammoth, polka, robot, vodka
Spanish	banana, breeze, cargo, couch, coyote, guitar, mosquito, ranch, rodeo, tequila, vanilla

✦ Different Alphabets

The Challenge

One of the biggest challenges for you as a tutor is to teach a student whose L1 does not use the Roman alphabet, as English does. Asian languages, Arabic languages, and languages using the Cyrillic alphabet are just a few examples. Although many students from those language backgrounds have some introduction to English, you might work with a student who is unfamiliar with the English writing system.

What Can You Do?

In teaching the alphabet, use books geared toward low-literacy adults (see Appendix A). The students will need some time to practice writing and forming letters as well as to learn about the sounds associated with them. Have students learn to write the words that they can use before having them learn to read and write words they do not know.

Being aware of the personal, cultural, and linguistic factors that help or hinder language acquisition will help you become a better tutor. You can use the student's strengths and tolerate and work with weaknesses.

Case Studies: Points of Interest

✦ Case Study 1

- The sponsors of the class for the Somali women have tried to accommodate the women's Moslem culture by allowing the women to have their own class, without men present.

- Ms. Freeman is aware of the women's group orientation and allows them to work together.

- She does not know much about the Somali language when she starts tutoring; however, as the class continues, she can detect the women's particular linguistic problems, and she works on them.

✦ Case Study 2

- Omar is an introvert who has had some difficulties in the regular class but who works well one-on-one with his tutor.

- Ms. Hawkins learns that he is a kinesthetic learner, as he has mentioned he likes doing things, not just listening.

- When Ms. Hawkins meets Omar's parents, she notices that they are very formal and maintain some of the cultural practices of their country, including their manner of dress.

✦ Case Study 3

- Ms. Rogers treats Kim Su in a professional manner. She realizes that Kim Su straddles two cultures and that her goals and her husband's goals are quite different.

- Ms. Rogers structures the sessions so that Kim Su can make choices and measure her progress.

- Ms. Rogers is aware of Kim Su's difficulty in speaking English in front of her husband and her reluctance to express opinions, and allows her to develop skills at her own pace.

Observe and Reflect

1. Think about how you would want a tutor to relate to you if you were in another country having to learn another language. Are you accommodating your student in the same way?

2. Think about your own learning strategies. Be aware that your student may not share your preferences. Do not force your own style on your student, but be sensitive to various learning styles.

Unit 3: Construct

Now that you know your student's needs and level, you are ready to construct lessons that will involve your student as much as possible. This unit will show you how to make a lesson plan, adapt it for the student's language level, and communicate with speakers of other languages. It will also show you how to find and make appropriate lessons on many topics and levels using Internet sources.

CHAPTER 7

"How do I make a lesson plan that is appropriate for my student?"

Set reasonable objectives; provide appropriate materials and activities.

What Is a Lesson Plan, and Why Do I Need One?

A lesson plan makes you a more effective tutor. It makes your job easier by helping you and the student stay on track. It gives your lesson organization, continuity, and credibility. It also provides you with more than one trick up your sleeve in case you are not getting the desired results right away.

A good lesson plan

- describes the goals of a lesson and the means of accomplishing those goals
- gives purpose and organization to the lesson and serves as a record of what you have done with the student
- documents the techniques that have been successful and unsuccessful with the student

Here is a general lesson-plan format that can be used in most tutoring situations. The reproducible Lesson Planning Sheet at the end of this chapter, which follows this format, may be useful in constructing plans. (See chapter 3 for the general structure of a tutoring session and general suggestions for introducing new material for any level or topic in pronunciation, listening and speaking, writing, reading, and grammar.)

1. *objectives:* State the skills you want your student to demonstrate by the end of your lesson.

2. *materials:* List all the items you and the student will need in performing the activities of the lesson.

3. *activities:* List sequentially all the activities you and the student will do to accomplish the goals of the lesson. The list may include some or all of these elements:
   - a warmup or review of old information
   - a presentation of new information
   - practice of the new information
   - a summary or review of the new information

4. *contingency plan:* Make a backup plan in case your original plan does not work as well as you expect.

5. *homework:* Note any work that you would like the student to do independently to show mastery of the material you have just taught.

6. *evaluation:* Write a few brief comments about how well the student performed and, possibly, activities that worked or did not work especially well with the student. Other ways to measure and record your student's success include giving the student an exercise or test taken from a textbook in class and keeping a list of skills that are checked off as the student masters them (see chapter 10).

> The Internet and some textbooks provide many ready-made lesson plans.

How Do I Make a Lesson Plan?

To create a lesson plan based on the guidelines above, consider your student's age and language level as well as the answers to these questions:

1. How much time do you have for the lesson?
2. What topic are you going to teach, and how can it be broken down into subtopics?
3. How much can you reasonably expect your student to learn about your topic in the amount of time available?

Suppose that your topic is the English alphabet, and you are working with an adult student. You would need to cover these topics:

1. saying the letters
   - vowels
     - names of the letters
     - sounds of the letters

- consonants
  - — names of the letters
  - — sounds of the letters
2. reading the letters
3. writing the letters
   - lowercase manuscript letters
   - uppercase manuscript letters

✦ Step 1: Form an Objective

Once you have broken the teaching of the alphabet down into subtopics, you can think about the first component of a lesson plan—a reasonable objective for the lesson. Each of the topics above might require a separate lesson. If your student has never had any English instruction before, you might need to spend an entire lesson on saying the letters of the alphabet. In fact, a student who cannot read or speak English will probably need several lessons to learn the names and sounds of the letters.

A good objective must also be specific. "The student will know some letters of the alphabet" is not a good objective because it leaves two questions unanswered: Which letters will the student know? How will the student show that knowledge?

State the goal as a behavior that is easy to observe. "Omar will be able to read his name" is not a good objective because it does not state how you will know he can read. "Omar will be able to identify the names and sounds of the letters of his first name when he hears them or sees them" is better because it states the observable skills Omar will demonstrate.

> The objective is a statement of what the student, not the tutor, will do. "I will teach some letters of the alphabet" is not a good objective because it does not tell how the student will show what has been learned. It states only what the tutor plans to do.

Example: Objective for a Lesson on the Alphabet

For a beginning-level adult student who is learning the alphabet, a reasonable, specific, student-oriented, observable objective might be

> The student will be able to say the names and sounds of the letters of her first name. She will be able to write her first name in manuscript.

> Be sure to choose reasonable objectives that will not overwhelm or discourage the student.

✦ Step 2: Select Appropriate Activities

Choose activities based on the student's age, level of English competency, cultural background, and learning style. For example, an energetic, beginning-level second grader who recognizes words but is not ready to produce them orally might need a total physical response activity like Simon Says to demonstrate comprehension of verbs such as *sit, stand,* and *walk*. However, an adult student at the beginning level might feel more comfortable pointing at stick figures on a dry-erase board to show mastery of the same words.

> Ask students what kinds of activities they like to do in school, and incorporate similar activities in your lesson plans.

Students who are learning a new language need constant reinforcement, so it is always appropriate to begin with a review of the previous lesson as a way of getting the student ready for new material. An easy way to do this is to go over homework. In presenting activities,

- Use visual aids (e.g., pictures, charts, outlines) whenever possible (see chapter 9).
- Try not to do all the talking, and get the student as involved as possible.
- Always give the student a written or oral activity to practice what you have presented—the more practice, the more you build the student's confidence and mastery.
- A few minutes before the end of your lesson, stop and summarize or review what you have done, even if you have not completed all you intended to in that session.

> You may want to write your activities on a dry-erase board and check them off as you do them.

Example: Activities for a Lesson on the Alphabet

To teach adults to write their first name in manuscript, select activities that have a practical value for the students. For example, instead of teaching the letters of the English alphabet in order, teach the students how to read and write their name first. The students will probably have to do this task on many occasions, and one of the advantages of one-on-one instruction is that you can personalize lessons for the student. Here is one possible list of activities for this lesson plan:

1. Write the student's first name on a board or piece of paper.
2. Ask if the student can say each letter in the name without help. (Help with the ones the student does not know.)
3. Help the student find the letters in the name on a chart showing both lower- and uppercase manuscript letters.

4. Show pictures of objects that begin with each letter of the student's name. Say the name of an object that begins with the first letter. Ask the student to repeat (e.g., *Halima* begins with *h*; ask the student to say *hand*).

5. Teach the student to say the name of the letter *h* and the sound that it makes.

6. Show the student how to write each letter of the name individually. Model the order of each letter stroke and the height of each letter.

✦ Step 3: Choose and Locate Appropriate Materials

Make a "grocery list" of everything you will need to accomplish your objective efficiently. Nothing is more embarrassing than to discover in the middle of a lesson that you do not have something critical to the success of your carefully laid-out plans. Never assume that the student will bring the things you need. Be sure to include items for your contingency plan.

Example: Materials for a Lesson on the Alphabet

To teach a lesson on the alphabet, you might need

- a chart with all the letters of the English alphabet printed in upper- and lowercase
- pictures of objects whose names begin with each of the letters of the student's first name
- several pieces of lined writing paper
- two pencils
- pipe cleaners
- sentences with words that begin with the letters of the student's name and pictures of some of the objects named in the sentences

> - If you are working with more than one student, write down the number of each item you will need.
> - Keep your student's age in mind. You probably would not want to use alphabet blocks with a high school student or an adult.

Often you can make the items you need for a lesson. For example, you can create your own chart of letters on a computer. You may be able to get some materials from a teacher at a local school, from a bookstore, or from the sources listed in Appendix A. It is always a good idea to use a few professionally made materials so that you will look professional.

✦ Step 4: Prepare a Contingency Plan

If your students resist an activity you have selected, be prepared to offer another. Do not blame yourself for this resistance; perhaps the students never performed that type of activity in their native culture. With that in mind, be sure your second plan includes a totally different kind of activity.

Example: Contingency Plan for a Lesson on the Alphabet

Suppose the student who is learning the alphabet cannot remember the names of the letters and gets them mixed up, or suppose the student already knows how to write his or her first name. Your contingency plan might be as follows:

- Make letters using something flexible, such as pipe cleaners, or make block-style letters and cut them out.
- In a magazine, look for words that begin with the letters you are teaching.
- Work on the last name or the name of one of the student's family members.
- Practice saying, reading, and writing the student's address.

✦ Step 5: Assign Homework

When you assign homework,

- Do one or two samples with the students to make sure that the homework is not too difficult for them to do by themselves and that they understand the instructions.
- Do not make the assignment too long. From time to time, ask your students how long they spent on it. Some students who are especially eager to learn, however, may ask for longer assignments.

Example: Homework for a Lesson on the Alphabet

As homework for the lesson on the alphabet, if your students understood your original lesson, you could have them write each letter 10 times. If you had to use your contingency plan, you could give the students a magazine article and ask them to circle at least two words beginning with each of the letters in the lesson.

✦ Step 6: Evaluate the Lesson

If you work with more than one student, jotting down a brief note about something that one student had trouble doing or did especially well can be very helpful. It is easy to forget these details if you let too much time pass before making notes.

Example: Evaluation for a Lesson on the Alphabet

Concerning the student learning the alphabet, you might write this evaluation:

> This student learned better by making letters with her hands. She had trouble learning the letters by listening and repeating.

How Do I Actually Teach a Lesson Plan?

✦ What to Say

If you are teaching for the first time, you may wonder what to say, especially when working with someone who speaks limited English. To help your student understand you,

- Speak clearly at a moderate pace, but maintain the natural rhythm of English.

- Use short, simple sentences (e.g., "This is a hand").

- Avoid pronouns (e.g., say "*The book* is in my hand" instead of "*It* is in my hand"), passive voice (e.g., say "The girl caught the bird" instead of "The bird was caught by the girl"), and complex sentences (e.g., say "The girl caught the bird. The bird was tired and hungry" instead of "The bird that the girl caught was tired and hungry").

- Ask questions that require only one-word answers (e.g., "Is this a hand?" "Yes [No]." "What country are you from?" "China.").

- Use visual aids whenever possible (see chapter 9).

- Teach your students to say "Please repeat" or "Slowly, please" when they do not understand.

- Do not raise your voice if the student does not understand you unless the student has a hearing problem. Your student may think you are angry.

- Be sure you can say your student's name, and be sure your student can say your name.

Example: A Lesson on the Alphabet

In the scenario below, Ms. Freeman, the tutor in Case Study 1, presents a lesson on the English alphabet to Halima, one of her Somali students. This lesson follows the outline of the activities in Step 2 above.

Ms. Freeman:	Hello, Halima. How are you today?
Halima:	Fine, thanks, Ms. Freeman. You, too?
Ms. Freeman:	Yes, I'm fine. Thank you, Halima. Your dress is very pretty. Is it silk?
Halima:	Yes, silk from Somalia. I make it. You like, I make you one.
Ms. Freeman:	That is very nice of you. Maybe we can make a dress together in an English lesson.
Halima:	I happy to!
Ms. Freeman:	Today we will talk about the English alphabet. [She points to the chart of lowercase letters.] Can you say these letters?
Halima:	No. I not read.
Ms. Freeman:	That's OK. We will practice the letters of your name today. [She points to Halima's name on the board.] This is your name in English. [She says each syllable slowly and points to each one as

Continued on p. 90

	she says it.] Ha-li-ma. [She points to Halima.] Now you say your name. [She points to each syllable again and says each one softly with Halima.] Ha-li-ma. Now let's say the letters of your name. [She points to the letter *H*.] This is capital *H*. Say *capital H*.
Halima:	Capeeta *H*.
Ms. Freeman:	[She points to the letter *a*.] Good! This is the letter *a*. Say *a*.
Halima:	*a*.
Ms. Freeman:	Good! [She points to the letter *l*.] This is the letter *l*. Say *l*.
Halima:	*l*.
Ms. Freeman:	[She points to the letter *i*.] This is the letter *i*. Say *i*.
Halima:	*i*.
Ms. Freeman:	[She points to the letter *m*.] This is the letter *m*. Say *m*.
Halima:	*m*.
Ms. Freeman:	[She points to the last letter *a*.] This is the letter *a* again. Say *a*.
Halima:	*a*.
Ms. Freeman:	Very good! Now let's say all the letters again. [She says a letter and gestures for Halima to repeat.]

Notice that Mrs. Freeman uses the same sequence to teach each letter: First, she points to a letter. Then she says, "This is the letter [*X*]. Then she says, "Say [*X*]. Following a pattern is especially helpful for beginning-level students. She also smiles and encourages Halima.

Ms. Freeman:	[She places the alphabet chart in front of Halima so that she can also see the letters of her name on the board. She points to the alphabet in lowercase.] Some of these letters are small. [She points to the alphabet in uppercase.] Some of these letters are big. The big letters are called *capital* letters. Look at the first letter of your name. [She points to the letter *H*.] Is this a small letter?
Halima:	No, it big letter.
Ms. Freeman:	Good! It's a capital *H*. Say *capital H*.
Halima:	Capeeta *H*.
Ms. Freeman:	[She points to the letter *a* in *Halima* and to the lowercase *a* on the chart.] Is this a capital letter?
Halima:	No, it small letter.
Ms. Freeman:	Good! It's a small *a*. Say *a*.
Halima:	*a*.
Ms. Freeman:	[She points to the letter *l* in Halima and on the lowercase chart.] Is this a capital letter?
Halima:	No, it small letter.
[Ms. Freeman proceeds in this way for all the letters of Halima's name.]

Continued on p. 91

Ms. Freeman:	Now let's say all the letters of your name. [Three times, Ms. Freeman points to each letter as she and Halima say it.] Capital H-a-l-i-m-a. [Ms. Freeman writes *Sharifa, Fatima,* and *Kherto,* the names of the other Somali women in Case Study 1, on the board to see if Halima can find her own name.
Ms. Freeman:	[She points to the name *Sharifa.*] Is this your name?
Halima:	I not read.
Ms. Freeman:	[She points to the name *Halima.*] Is this your name?
Halima:	Halima.
Ms. Freeman:	Good! This is your name, Halima.

Although Halima did not understand Ms. Freeman's question, she knew that Ms. Freeman was pointing to her name. This confirmation is all Ms. Freeman needs to be sure that Halima can now read her name.

[Ms. Freeman notices that she has only a few minutes to complete her lesson with Halima. She realizes that she will not have time to teach Halima to write her name today. She does a quick activity to reinforce Halima's ability to recognize the letters of her name.]

Ms. Freeman:	[She gives Halima a piece of paper with a sentence written on it. There are also six labeled pictures of a girl named Hannah, five apples, two lemons, a gallon of ice cream, a box of mushrooms, and three apricots.] Hannah bought apples, lemons, ice cream, mushrooms, and apricots at the grocery store.[She points to the *a* in apples.] Is this a capital *H*?
Halima:	[She shakes her head.]
Ms. Freeman:	Good! [She points to the *i* in ice cream.] Is this a capital *H*?
Halima:	[She shakes her head.]
Ms. Freeman:	Good! [She points to the *H* in Hannah.] Is this a capital *H*?
Halima:	Capital *H*.
Ms. Freeman:	Yes! [She underlines the *H*.] This is a capital *H*. [She points to the letter *a* in apples.] Is this the letter *a*?
Halima:	*a*.
Ms. Freeman:	Good! [She underlines the letter *a*.] This is the letter *a*.

[Ms. Freeman proceeds in this manner until she has underlined each letter of Halima's name. Then she shows how these letters spell Halima's name and points to each letter:

  *H*annah bought *a*pples, *l*emons, *i*ce cream, *m*ushrooms, and *a*pricots at the grocery store.

  H   a   l   i   m   a

  These are the letters of your name. Say *Halima*.

Continued on p. 92

Halima:	Halima.
Ms. Freeman:	Now say the names of the letters. [She points to the first letter and helps Halima by saying "Capital [X]." Then she waits to see if Halima can say the letters by herself as she points to each letter.]
Halima:	H-a-l-i-ma.
Ms. Freeman:	You have done very good work today, Halima. Very good! [She smiles at Halima and claps her hands to be sure Halima knows she has done well.] Now you can read your name! Next time you will learn to write your name. I will see you next week. Thank you for your hard work. Good-bye, Halima.
Halima:	Bye-bye, Ms. Freeman. Thank you!

Ms. Freeman decides not to give Halima any homework until she can write her name. She will teach Halima to do this in the next lesson. Ms. Freeman can use the sentence and pictures from the end of this lesson to teach Halima to recognize additional letters, read and write additional words, and learn numbers in future lessons.

How Can I Make Lesson Plans for Different Skills and Levels?

If you are tutoring students in more than one language skill, you may find that they are more proficient in one skill than in another. For example, a student may be at the beginning level in speaking but at the intermediate level in reading.

When you begin to tutor, pay close attention to the students' response to the material you use. If they fidget and watch the clock, they may be bored and unchallenged, and may need higher level activities. On the other hand, if they look confused and have difficulty with your activities, you may need to lower the level of your presentation. If the students are totally engaged in your class and act surprised when the class is over, you have undoubtedly chosen just what they need.

Pace your lesson to match the level of the students:

- For beginners, keep the lesson simple and give much reinforcement.
- For intermediate-level students, find materials that interest and challenge but do not overwhelm them.
- Most important of all, do not do all the talking, and encourage questions. Also be sure to smile and offer encouragement even when your students make mistakes.

Below are model lesson plans on specific topics. The abbreviations in parentheses, which indicate the language level of the lesson, are used to indicate the level of materials in many ESL materials catalogues: low beginning (LB), beginning (B), high beginning (HB), low intermediate (LI), intermediate (I), high intermediate (HI), low advanced (LA), and advanced (A).

One lesson often builds on another. In the lesson examined in this chapter, Ms. Freeman, the tutor in Case Study 1, did not have time to teach Halima how to write her name in manuscript. In her plan for the next lesson, shown below, Ms. Freeman will review what she has covered and use that knowledge to present new information.

Objective

Halima will be able to write her name in manuscript.

Materials

manuscript alphabet chart of upper- and lowercase letters, individual cutout manuscript letters, pencil with eraser, lined writing paper, pipe cleaners, magazines

Activities

1. Review the reading of the letters of Halima's name in manuscript.
2. Ask Halima to find the letters of her name on an alphabet chart and circle them. Be sure to include any letter(s) in uppercase.
3. Present the cutout letters of Halima's name, and arrange them in the correct order to spell her name. Ask her to name each letter as you place it down.
4. Mix up the letters. Ask Halima to put them back into the correct order.
5. Use the eraser end of a pencil to trace the letters of Halima's name on the alphabet chart. Each time you trace one letter, have Halima trace it after you and say the name of the letter.
6. Determine whether Halima is left-handed or right-handed. Show her how to hold the pencil correctly in her writing hand.
7. Model the writing of the first letter of her name on a piece of paper:
    *   Ask her to trace the letter with the eraser end of the pencil.
    *   Ask her to write the letter with the pencil end. Be sure to point out where to begin and end each stroke of the letter.
    *   Have her write the letter at least five times.
8. Repeat Step 7 for each letter of her name.
9. Write Halima's name on her writing paper. Ask her to write her name five times.

Contingency Plan

Halima can hold the pencil correctly but has trouble duplicating the shapes of the letters.

Continued on p. 94

---

1. Ask her to make the shapes of the letters with pipe cleaners and trace them with her fingers.
2. Find a magazine with large print. Help her find words that begin with the letters of her name.

Homework

- (for original lesson) Ask Halima to write her first name 10 times.
- (for contingency plan) Write Halima's name 5 times on a piece of paper. Ask her to trace each name 2 times with the writing end of a pencil.

Evaluation

Halima needs more practice writing the letters of her first name before she learns to write other letters. She sometimes had trouble forming the letters because she held the pencil too tightly.

✦ A Lesson Plan for Intermediate- to Advanced-Level Writing (I–A)

Adult ESL students often need help with such tasks as writing checks and filling out forms to apply for a job, open a bank account, or order from a catalogue. You can easily obtain sample forms at your local bank or department store or even on the Internet. Your student may also need to write different types of letters, such as a complaint letter asking for replacement of a damaged or faulty product, a cover letter for a job application, or an informal letter to an American. In a lesson on writing such a letter (shown below), you would teach the correct heading, greeting, tone, and closing.

Objective

Katrina will complete a letter of complaint using a correct business format.

Materials

model complaint letter (written by the teacher or obtained from the Internet, a writing handbook for adults, or a grammar book),writing paper, pens, correction fluid, computer or dry-erase board and markers, address of the company to which the student is writing, model number of the defective product, receipt for the product, business envelope, stamps, telephone book, picture dictionary or catalogue

Activities

1. Label the parts of the model letter (*heading, date, greeting, body, closing,* and *signature*).

Continued on p. 95

2. Discuss the purpose of the model letter (e.g., the writer wants to get a refund for a defective product or exchange it for a new one).

3. Discuss the tone of the model letter (i.e., the language is formal and businesslike).

4. List the defects of the product the student would like to exchange.

5. List the results the student would like to obtain from the letter.

6. Begin to write each part of the letter on the board or computer using the model letter as a guide.

Contingency Plan

Katrina has forgotten to bring the company's address and cannot describe the problem she is having with the product.

- Find a picture of the product in a catalogue or picture dictionary, and ask your student to point at the part of the product that does not work.

- If your student is artistic, have him or her draw a picture to demonstrate.

Homework

- Ask Katrina to complete a rough draft of the letter and bring it to the next class to correct grammar and spelling.

Evaluation

Katrina's rough draft of the letter shows certain grammar and spelling problems. These problems will be the focus of other lessons.

✦ A Lesson Plan for Pronunciation and Speaking (HB–A)

When teaching pronunciation, check on sounds that may be especially difficult for speakers of your student's first language. For example, Spanish speakers often have difficulty hearing the difference between the long vowel sound of *ee* in *sheep* and the short vowel sound of *i* in *ship*. A book such as *Learner English* (Swan & Smith, 2001) can help you identify these problem areas for speakers of many different languages. Some Web sites contain helpful information, too (see Appendix A).

When teaching beginning-level students, you may discover great reluctance even to try to pronounce English sounds. If this should happen, try using activities such as the game Simon Says so your student can use a physical response instead of a verbal response to show understanding of English. Another way to help reluctant speakers is to teach songs, rhymes, or poems that illustrate the rhythm of English. Graham's *Jazz Chants* (1978, 2001) provide helpful materials for teaching grammar, vocabulary, and pronunciation simultaneously to speakers of all ages.

The following lesson plan for teaching a specific English sound could be adapted to fit the needs of students of various levels and ages.

Objective

Juan will

- be able to place his tongue between his teeth to produce the voiceless sound represented by *th* at the beginning, middle, and end of words
- begin to monitor his pronunciation of this sound to determine when he is not saying it correctly.

Materials

printed nursery rhymes, selected words with voiceless *th* sound, mirror, paper, audiotape player/recorder, blank audiotape

1. Recite a nursery rhyme.
2. Say words with voiceless *th* at the beginning, middle, or end (e.g., *thought, ether, both*).
3. Show the student how to place his tongue between his teeth to say *th*. Have the student use a mirror to be sure he is placing his tongue in the correct position after you model it for him.
4. Say *th* words individually, in sentences, and in a song.

Contingency Plan

Juan has difficulty remembering to place his tongue between his teeth.

5. Ask him to hold a piece of paper in front of his mouth. Have him put his tongue between his teeth and blow so that the paper moves.
6. Ask him to keep the paper in front of his mouth and say a *th* word, such as *think*. The paper should move every time he says the word correctly.

Homework

Have Juan underline all the *th* words in a reading passage, read the passage aloud, and record it on audiotape.

Evaluation

Juan had difficulty remembering to place his tongue between his teeth to say *th*.

If your student wants to learn conversation skills, choose an ESL text that uses the communicative approach (see Appendix A). This text will provide you and your student with true-to-life dialogues and other practical speaking activities.

✦ A Lesson Plan for Grammar (LI-A)

When you teach grammar, it is always helpful to do a background check to determine the common pitfalls for students from a particular country who are learning English. For example, Chinese students (e.g., Kim Su, the student in Case Study 3) often have difficulty remembering to add *-ed* to an English verb in the past tense because in Chinese verbs do not change to indicate a different time. As a result, Chinese students might say, "Yesterday I walk to the store."

This lesson plan includes a time frame for each activity. Sometimes, allotting a certain number of minutes to each activity can keep your lesson moving at a good pace.

Objectives

Kim Su will
1. demonstrate the ability to distinguish between verbs that double the final consonant before adding *-ed* and those that do not.
2. be able to distinguish between the /t/ sound of *-ed* at the end of words like *shopped* and the /d/ sound of *-ed* at the end of words like *robbed*.

Materials

paragraph with blank spaces left for regular past tense verbs, paper, pen, audiotape player/recorder, blank audiotape, list of regular verbs, dry-erase board and markers, audiotape of speakers saying past tense verbs, timer, handout with questions about yesterday's activities, interactive grammar book

Activities
1. Give Kim Su the paragraph with blank spaces left for past tense verbs. Have her write the correct past tense forms. Have Kim Su read the paragraph with the correct verb forms, and record it on audiotape. (15 minutes)
2. Practice doubling the final consonant on one-syllable verbs that end with one vowel and one consonant before adding *-ed*. Ask Kim Su to locate such verbs in a mixed list written on the dry-erase board. (15 minutes)
3. Listen to speakers on an audiotape saying past tense verbs ending in *-ed* sounding like /d/ and /t/, and ask Kim Su to distinguish between the two sounds. (15 minutes)

Continued on p. 98

4. Ask Kim Su questions about what she did yesterday. Have her respond in complete sentences using the past tense. (15 minutes)

Contingency Plan

Kim Su has difficulty saying the final *-ed* sounds and recognizing when to double the final consonant.

- Use a song or rhyme (e.g., the jazz chant "A Bad Day" in Graham, 1978) that focuses on past tense *-ed*.
- Assign an exercise from the grammar book that requires Kim Su to apply rules for doubling the final consonant before adding *-ed*.

Homework

Give Kim Su a handout with the same questions she answered orally in Step 4. Ask her to write the answers to the questions to form a paragraph.

Evaluation

- Kim Su had difficulty remembering to double the final consonant of one-syllable regular verbs. She does not pronounce the *-ed* sound when speaking.
- (tutor's self-evaluation) I needed more activities to help Kim Su understand when to double the final consonant before adding *-ed*.

Beginning teachers and tutors of grammar are sometimes tempted to cover too many topics in a lesson. Always narrow your topic so that you can cover every aspect of it thoroughly in one lesson. By limiting the topic, Kim Su's tutor covers the grammar, pronunciation, and spelling of past tense verbs ending with *-ed*.

✦ A Lesson Plan for Reading (LI–HI)

Reading is one of the best ways to develop all language skills. However, language learners are not always motivated to read because it is so difficult for them. One way to motivate students is to find reading material on subjects that interest them and provide materials that appeal to your student's age group.

Good materials are available for beginning-level adults. They do not have to read the same materials you would give to a 6-year-old. Libraries, literacy councils, and ESL catalogues will help you find *high/low reading materials,* which have a high level of interest at a low level of English. Many classic and universally appealing pieces of literature have been simplified so that readers of all English levels can read and enjoy them.

The lesson plan below, for a low intermediate–level reader, could be adapted for readings at various levels. For example, a beginning-level student needs shorter readings with simple grammar and vocabulary, illustrations, and fewer words on a page. Such readings are less intimidating. Comprehension questions should require only one word to answer. Students might need to consult a picture dictionary for some vocabulary. Intermediate-level students can answer more difficult *why* and *how* questions in phrases and short sentences and can use a monolingual ESL dictionary. They can understand more complex vocabulary and sentence structure but still benefit from illustrations and prereading activities.

Objectives

Ahmed will

1. be able to determine the meaning of new vocabulary from the context of the reading and by using a dictionary

2. become aware of cultural differences

3. show understanding of the story by answering comprehension questions

Materials

two copies of an adapted version of "The Necklace" (e.g., de Maupassant, 1907/ 1996, pp. 71–87), pencil, dry-erase board and markers, dictionary

Activities

1. Preview the story by looking at the pictures, reading captions under the pictures, and reading the headings and study questions.

2. Predict what the story is about.

3. List the names of the three main characters on the dry-erase board and briefly identify each one (i.e., Mme. Mathilde Loisel, a French woman; M. Loisel, her husband; Mme. Forrestier, a friend).

4. Discuss the story's background (e.g., "The story takes place in France in the 1800s. It was written by the famous French writer, Guy de Maupassant. The names of the characters are French and do not look or sound like English names. The story talks about the cost of something in French *francs*. There are approximately 5 francs to 1 U.S. dollar.")

5. Read the story aloud. (Ask the student if he prefers to listen or would like to take turns reading. Sometimes students enjoy taking the part of one of the characters.) Ask the student to underline words he does not understand, but do not stop to explain them.

6. Ask a few questions to see if the student understands the main points (e.g., Why doesn't Mathilde want to go to the party at first? What did her husband want to buy with the money for Mathilde's dress? What did the

Continued on p. 100

Loisels do to pay for a new necklace? How long did it take them? Does this story teach a lesson?).

7. Discuss the vocabulary words that the student underlined. Help him try to figure out the meaning from their context. Show him how to use a dictionary for the pronunciation and the meaning of the words. Point out special features of the words he underlined. For example, *shabbiness, dinginess,* and *ugliness* are all nouns ending with the suffix *-ness*.

8. Relate the story to the student's life by asking questions like the following: Have you ever lost something valuable? How did you feel? Did you find it? Do you think it is a good idea to borrow something you cannot afford to buy?

Contingency Plan

Be prepared to discuss and compare the concept of borrowing in France, in the United States, and in the student's native country:

- Is it common to borrow in all three countries?
- What should a person do if the borrowed item is lost?
- How long should a person keep something that is borrowed?
- Is it acceptable to borrow from a relative or a friend?

Homework

Write a paragraph to answer this question: Do you think Mme. and M. Loisel did the right thing by not telling Mme. Forrestier the necklace was lost? Explain.

Evaluation

The student was upset about the concept of borrowing in the story because this behavior is not accepted in his native country. He needs more readings that will help him understand cultural differences.

Learn something about the culture of the student you are teaching so that you are aware of differences and similarities between that culture and the culture depicted in the reading, and topics to which your student might be sensitive. Try to find English stories about the student's culture.

International students sometimes need help preparing for standardized tests, such as the Test of English as a Foreign Language (TOEFL©) and the Test of Spoken English (TSE©) (see Appendix B). Bookstores carry a number of excellent preparation guides for most standardized tests. Although these guides are generally designed to be used as self-tutoring devices, many students want to work with an instructor who can answer questions and teach areas of weakness. Generally these texts present a diagnostic test and suggest a plan of study that is helpful to you and the student. Be sure the student understands the following information about the test:

- length (i.e., the time allotted and the number of questions)
- types of questions (i.e., subject areas and response methods)
- method of scoring (e.g., there are no extra deductions for wrong answers on the TOEFL, so students may guess on difficult questions)
- the time and place of testing
- materials and documentation required (e.g., social security number, identification card)
- cost and accepted methods of payment
- method of registration
- rules and restrictions for taking the test

After covering these basics, use the regular lesson plan format to teach a specific topic, as in the lesson plan below.

Objective

Gita will be able to recognize gerunds (i.e., nouns ending *-ing*) in readings and use them in writing.

Materials

ESL grammar text, TOEFL preparation book, pencil

Activities

1. Review the uses of nouns in sentences.
2. Substitute some of the nouns in these sentences with gerunds.
3. Underline *-ing* words in a paragraph. Find the ones that are used as subjects and objects; note that these are gerunds.
4. Have Gita find *-ing* words in another paragraph and tell which ones are gerunds.
5. Have Gita do a sample TOEFL preparation exercise on gerunds.

Continued on p. 102

Contingency Plan

If Gita confuses gerunds with *-ing* verbs and participles, use some exercises in the ESL grammar textbook to help her see the difference.

Homework

Have Gita write a paragraph about sports whose names are gerunds, such as *skiing, swimming,* and *skating.* Ask her to underline each gerund in the paragraph and tell if it is a subject or object.

Evaluation

Gita could identify gerunds in the readings in class but had difficulty identifying the gerunds in her paragraph.

✦ A Lesson Plan for a Nonliterate Student (LB)

Some students, perhaps adult refugees from a third-world country, can neither read nor write in their native language. Such students will need the same kind of help you had when you first learned to write. They will not know how to position the paper on a desk or how to hold a pencil. You may have to play a game that will show you if they are left-handed or right-handed.

The lesson plans that Ms. Freeman used to teach Halima to read and write her name would suit this situation. In addition to writing their name, adult ESL students should learn to read, write, and say numbers (as taught in the lesson plan below). No matter what you teach beginning-level nonliterate students, be sure to use many pictures and realia.

Objectives

Raymond will
1. be able to read, write, and say the numbers 0–10
2. respond to the question *How many?* by counting and telling the correct number of objects
3. show understanding of the words for the objects he counts by putting them into a bag when told to do so

Continued on p. 103

Materials

10 of each of the following: paper clips, pencils, pennies, dimes, nickels, quarters, buttons, pencils, paper bags, paper cups, pieces of candy, index cards; small dry-erase board and markers; dry eraser; number flash cards; paper; pencil; homework handout with pictures of objects to count; deck of cards

Activities

1. Hold up one hand. Point at your fingers and say, "These are fingers. How many fingers?" Count the fingers on that hand. Hold up your other hand, and continue counting to 10.

2. Ask Raymond to hold up his hands. Point at his fingers and say, "These are fingers. How many fingers?" Count his fingers.

3. Count out a different number of each kind of object. Put the objects of each kind in separate bags. Leave one bag empty. Ask Raymond to take out and count the number of objects in each bag.

4. Write each number on the board. Say it as you write it. Ask Raymond to repeat each number after you.

5. Point at each number in order and say it. Ask Raymond to repeat after you. Do this several times. Point at each number (without saying it), and ask him to say it.

6. Point at each number randomly, and ask Raymond to say it.

7. Hold up the number flash cards in order. Ask Raymond to say the number on each card. Mix up the cards and repeat.

8. Tell Raymond to put a certain number of the small objects into each bag, using a different number for each bag (e.g., "Put eight quarters in the bag.").

9. Write the numbers 0–10 in a column on a piece of paper. Trace the number with the eraser end of a pencil. Ask Raymond to do the same. Write the number on the paper with the pencil end, and ask him do the same five times. Use this same procedure for each number.

Contingency Plan

- If Raymond has trouble writing with a pencil, ask him to write on the dry-erase board.

- If he cannot say the numbers, let him point at the correct number after you say it.

- If he learns quickly, play a game of Go Fish.

Continued on p. 104

- Have Raymond write each number 10 times.
- Ask him to count the pictures on the handout and write the correct number.

Evaluation

Vocabulary for the objects was difficult for the student.

✦ A Content Area Lesson Plan (LI-HI)

At times a student may need help in a content area, such as history or social studies. For example, an eighth-grade Japanese student who is taking a world history course in a U.S. classroom may come to you with a reading assignment that seems easy to you but is insurmountable to him because of the vocabulary and information he is expected to read, understand, and remember for a possible quiz the next day. In this case, follow the reading lesson plan described in A Lesson Plan for Reading above, which includes prereading activities that greatly enhance comprehension. If possible, obtain a copy of the content to be covered before you meet with the student so you can prepare ahead of time and will not have to look for information during the lesson.

Content to Cover

A Global History (Stavrianos, Andrews, McLane, Safford, & Sheridan, 1979), chapter 5, "Europe Unites the World: 1500–1763," pages 76–79

Objectives
1. language: Makiko will be able to match pictures to words for the following vocabulary: *horse-drawn carriage, steamship, locomotive, propeller airplane, jet airplane, telegraph, telephone, television, satellite.*
2. content areas: She will be able to name improvements in transportation and communication from 1400 to 1900.
3. thinking skills: She will be able to use adjectives to compare and contrast old methods of transportation and communication with modern ones.

Materials

outline of main points of the text (with some words missing), pictures (from a clip art collection or from the Internet) mounted on index cards illustrating methods of transportation and communication listed under "language" above, map of the world, dry-erase board with vocabulary words and time line, markers, ESL dictionary, text or encyclopedia for younger student that covers the same topic

Continued on p. 105

Activities

1. With Makiko, look at the illustrations and charts on the assigned pages.

2. Have Makiko read the captions under the pictures and charts, and the words in boldface.

3. Ask her to fill in the missing words on the outline.

4. Have her match the pictures on the index cards to vocabulary written on the dry-erase board.

5. Ask her to compare an old method of transportation with a modern one by finding adjectives on the dry-erase board that describe each method.

6. Have her match each flash card of a mode of transportation to the correct year on the time line and the correct place on the map.

Contingency Plan

If Makiko still seems overwhelmed by the English in her textbook, do the following:

- Use a text or an encyclopedia for a younger student that covers the same topic.
- Create a graphic organizer on transportation (see chapter 9).

Evaluation

Makiko found it difficult to locate the information needed to fill in the outline. She had no problems matching pictures to vocabulary or finding adjectives to describe the pictures. She enjoyed comparing old ways with new ways and did so very accurately.

Additional Tips for Lesson Planning

The lesson plans above are designed to show you what plans for lessons in the different language skills look like. You should also refer to the formats for tutoring sessions in each language skill given in chapter 3. Below are a few more effective techniques you can use.

◆ Reading

- If your student is studying literature in a mainstream classroom and has trouble understanding it, you can
    — look for a summary in the Cliff Notes or Monarch Notes series of literature study guides

- look for a simplified version of the work in an ESL catalogue

- paraphrase or summarize the story by writing one or two sentences about the main idea of each page of the reading

- If the chapters in the reading have no titles, help your student create titles that give the main topic of each chapter.

- Have the student underline or highlight unfamiliar words, look each word up in a dictionary, put a dot next to the word in the dictionary, and put another dot next to the word every time the student has to look it up.

- Have the student keep a notebook of new words that includes a division of the word into syllables, the part of speech (e.g., noun, verb), a definition, and a sentence using the word.

- Record on audiotape your student's answers to questions about his or her background. Use the answers to create a reading. (See the second point under Writing below.)

✦ Writing

- Begin a dialogue journal:

  1. Write a letter asking questions you would like the student to answer in a letter back to you.

  2. Tell the student to answer the letter and to end it with at least one question the student wants you to answer, even if the questions are the same ones you asked.

  3. Continue the dialogue by ending your letter with a question.

  Do not call attention to grammar and spelling errors by making corrections on the student's letters. Instead, put a question mark next to something you do not understand, or model the correct grammar in your next letter. The idea is to make your student learn to write without being afraid to make mistakes.

- Help your student write about a topic by asking guided questions. For example, the following questions will guide a student to write a paragraph about his or her family:

  1. What is your name?

  2. Where are you from?

  3. Do you come from a large or a small family?

  4. How many people are in your family?

  5. What are the names of the people in your family and how are they related to you?

  6. Do you have any pets? What kind?

  7. What does your family like to do for fun?

✦ Grammar

- Use the mistakes your student has made in writing a paragraph (e.g., the one above) as the basis of a grammar lesson. For example, a student who writes "My name José. I from Spain" in answer to the first two questions does not know how to use the verb *be* in sentences. Locate a lesson for the student in a grammar book or on the Internet, or create a lesson of your own if you feel comfortable doing so.

- Give practice in using a grammar point the student has learned by using questions and sentences related to the student's own life. For example, if your student has a brother, practice different types of information questions by asking, "How old is your brother?" "Does your brother play any sports?" "Do you and your brother like to do things together?"

✦ Listening, Speaking, and Pronunciation

- Select a short reading, and make two copies of it. As a student reads it aloud, mark
  - sounds the student has difficulty pronouncing
  - stress placed on the wrong syllable or syllables left out
  - lack of pauses after commas and end marks, such as periods or semicolons

Do not try to correct all the students' mistakes at once. Work on one problem at a time until the students begin to catch the mistakes, too. If they have trouble hearing the sound, have them watch you say the sound and then check in a mirror to be sure they are moving their mouth and tongue in the same way.

- Ask your students to choose a good speaker of English on television as a model of how they would like to sound and to watch this person for 15 minutes every day.

- Encourage your students to practice conversation skills with at least one native speaker of English. Have the students write down in a notebook specific times when they could not understand English or could not express what they wanted to say (e.g., ordering food in a restaurant, trying to get help finding something in a store, talking about football with an American friend). Use these problem situations as the basis of a class. For example, find an article about football in the newspaper and discuss words like *pass, fumble, touchdown, field goal,* and *offensive foul.*

- With your students, play the parts of characters in a story, a play, or even a comic book. (Comic books are a great source of vocabulary, U.S. cultural topics, and idioms, and the pictures help make the meaning clear.)

The lessons in this chapter are just a starting point; they are not written in stone. Do not be afraid to use your own ideas as you get to know what your students need and what works best for them.

Case Studies: Points of Interest

✦ Case Study 1

- Ms. Freeman uses a variety of activities to reinforce her lesson and hold the interest of her students.

- She paces her activities quickly enough that students can learn but are not bored.

✦ Case Study 2

- For her contingency plan, Ms. Hawkins is careful to select a story that will interest a boy Omar's age. Although she does not use this activity, she has it available for a future lesson.

- Ms. Hawkins' objective is not directly related to the lesson she teaches. However, gaining Omar's trust is important for her success in future lessons.

✦ Case Study 3

- Ms. Rogers in essence has three contingency plans: She is prepared to teach Kim Su pronunciation on three different levels.

- Ms. Rogers makes sure that Kim Su has reasonable expectations for improving her pronunciation.

> All three tutors made immediate evaluations of their students to help them with future lesson plans. They were all well prepared and gave the impression of being caring, knowledgeable professionals.

Observe and Reflect

1. How would you rate the lesson plans of the tutors in the three case studies: *excellent, good, average,* or *poor*?

2. Were all three tutors successful in presenting their lessons? Why or why not? What criteria would you use to determine their success?

3. Identify the six steps of a lesson plan in Ms. Freeman's lesson to Halima on the letters of her name. (See the section How Do I Actually Teach a Lesson Plan?)

4. Which tutor had to use a more general lesson plan until she had a chance to meet with her student?

Lesson Planning Sheet

Objectives

Materials

Activities

Contingency Plan

Homework

Evaluation

CHAPTER 8

"How can I use the Internet in my lessons?"

Search ESL Web sites for materials, lessons, and activities geared to the students' age, language level, and language skill.

What ESL Topics Can I Find on the Internet?

You can find information on almost any topic relevant to you, your student, and your tutoring sessions on the Internet. You can download most of these materials for immediate use as long as you observe the copyright notices on the site and do not violate copyright law by using the materials for personal profit. Following are some of the topics you can find on the Internet.

- methods of teaching ESL
- ESL lesson plans
- ESL textbooks
- activities for teaching ESL
- games for teaching ESL
- songs for teaching ESL

- ESL grammar, reading, writing, listening/speaking, and pronunciation
- ESL for children, teenagers, and adults
- ESL for grade school, high school, and college/university students
- ESL for illiterate adults
- ESL in content areas
- ESL quizzes and tests
- assessment of ESL students
- ESL picture and word dictionaries
- graphic organizers

> If you do not have a computer or Internet access in your home or office, look in your local library. Many public libraries have computer stations with Internet access available for use.

How Can I Find What I'm Looking For?

To find information on a specific topic, visit one of the Web sites listed in Appendix A or do a search for one of the topics listed above with your favorite search engine (e.g., *Yahoo!,* http://www.yahoo.com; *Google,* http://www.google.com; *HotBot,* http://hotbot.lycos.com; *AltaVista,* http://www.altavista.com; *Excite,* http://www.excite.com; or *Lycos,* http://www.lycos.com). The Web addresses (known as *uniform resource locators,* or URLs) for the sites listed here and in Appendix A are current as of the time of publication. Web sites change addresses from time to time. If the change is recent, the old site will sometimes include a link to the new site, which you can then add to your list of bookmarked sites.

> The sites described here and in Appendix A are just a sample of what is available on the Internet. Some sites may require a certain browser in order to access them, and some shut down from time to time to be updated. Do not be discouraged if you cannot access a site; there are plenty of sites to choose from.

How Can I Use These Sites in My Tutoring?

Internet resources can save you time and money and can make your lessons professional and efficient. Following are a few suggestions:

- If you find a lesson you want to use, make a hard copy of the materials to use for the activities (see chapter 7 on making lesson plans), or if the site allows copying for personal use, make a copy for yourself and each student in your class to use as a textbook or workbook.

- Find and follow a ready-made sequence of lessons in which one lesson builds upon the previous lesson, becoming gradually more difficult as the student advances. For example, you could follow Pearson Adult Learning Centre's (2002a) schedule of basic composition lessons from January through May, teaching your lessons in the same order (not necessarily on the same dates) and using Pearson's materials.

- Use an online exercise in grammar or vocabulary to supplement or review a lesson on a topic you have already taught. You may choose to make a hard copy of the exercise or let the student do it on the computer.

- Use online exercises to refresh your own memory about a particular topic in grammar or writing.

- Assign an Internet activity to your student as homework, or use it as a warmup or review activity for your next class.

- Make a note of sites that contain reference materials you can use to prepare for or teach a lesson (e.g., online dictionaries, writing texts, or encyclopedias).

- Use the Internet to accommodate your student's interests. For example, if a student is interested in photography or rock climbing, do an Internet search for articles on these topics.

What Are Some Good Sites for Tutors of Adult ESL Learners?

✦ *Adult Education ESL Teachers Guide* (Graham & Walsh, 1996; http://humanities.byu.edu/elc/teacher/TeacherGuideMain)

Audience

beginning-level, intermediate-level, and illiterate adults

Special Features
- answers to basic questions about the adult ESL student, for example,
  — What are some of the major problems that ESL learners have with vocabulary?
  — What are some of the major problems that ESL learners have with grammar?
  — What are some important things to know about pronunciation?
- information on oral and literary assessment.
- a teacher education module for each lesson on grammar and vocabulary. For example, Section 2 for the beginning level includes tutor's instructions plus printable lessons and activities on the following topics:
  — greetings and introductions
  — ordering food
  — filling out forms
  — calling on the phone

- personal information
- shopping for clothes
- asking about classroom objects
- telling the date
- telling time
- visiting the doctor
- finding a job

Site Sample: Listening/Speaking/Vocabulary (Beginning Level)

The site sample in Figure 1 is from a beginning-level lesson in listening, speaking, and vocabulary. To use the sample with a student, you might use the following procedure:

1. Read the entire dialogue to your student.

2. Read the dialogue again, with you and your student playing the two roles.

3. Read the dialogue again, switching roles with your student.

4. Give your student the commands in Practice 1. If the student cannot read or follow them, say them and act them out yourself. (This activity is a *total physical response* [TPR] activity, in which the student responds by doing rather than speaking.)

5. Repeat the commands until the student can follow them all. Mix up the commands if possible. If you do not have the required furniture in your classroom, put the pictures from the lesson around the room to represent the furniture.

6. Say the words of a command. Then ask your student to repeat it after you. Help with words that are difficult for the student to pronounce.

7. Ask the student to give you the commands.

8. Put various objects, such as your book, pencil, pen, and folder, in various places in your room. (If you do not have a desk, bookcase, and file cabinet, write the words on the pictures of those objects.) Play the game in Practice 7 of the site sample.

9. With your student, take turns asking and answering questions about where various objects are located, as in Practice 8 of the site sample.

Notice that three of the online lessons given here use graphic organizers to help students break down information into understandable chunks (see chapter 9). All of the samples can be used for one-on-one or small-group tutoring and could be adapted for various age groups.

Figure 1. Site Sample From Adult Education ESL Teachers Guide

Lesson 4: Asking About Classroom Objects

[includes pictures of a desk, a file cabinet, and a bookcase with books]

Objective: To be able to ask for the whereabouts of personal belongings.
To be able to identify the locations of objects in the classroom.

Dialog:

T: Where's my book?
S: I don't know. Look on the shelf.
T: Which shelf?
S: Try the top one.
T: It's not there.
S: Check in the desk drawer.
T: Here it is. Thanks.

Practice 1: Commands, Listen and Do

Stand up.
Go over to the book stand.
Look on the top shelf.
Go over to the filing cabinet.
Look in the bottom drawer.
Go over to the desk.
Check in the middle drawer.
Go back to your seat.
Sit down.

[Practices 2–6 reinforce the vocabulary from Practice 1.]

Practice 7: Game

The teacher closes her eyes and asks:
T: Where's my _____?
S: Look under the desk.
T: It's not there.
S: Try on the shelf.
T: Which shelf?
S: The _____ one.

Practice 8: Vocabulary Expansion

Where's my   book?   folder?   pen?
                  pencil? watch?

✦ *ESL Lounge* (http://www.esl-lounge.com)

Target Audience

adults of all levels; texts and magazines for younger students also listed

Special Features
- description of each level from beginning to advanced
- free, printable lesson plans and materials for grammar, vocabulary, reading, and pronunciation
- an *ESL Books Guide* that includes the following topics:
  — teacher theory and practice
  — games, warmers, and other short activities
  — pronunciation, speaking, and listening activities
  — grammar reference
  — music in the class
  — grammar practice activities
  — dictionaries
  — composition and writing
  — reading and vocabulary
  — business English
  — reference books for idioms, phrasal verbs, collocations, and other topics

Site Sample: Vocabulary (Preintermediate Level)

To use the site sample shown in Figure 2 for activities in a lesson, follow these steps:

1. Bring to the session pictures, perhaps in a picture dictionary, to show the meaning of each vocabulary word. If you have time, put each word and each picture on a separate card, or ask your student to help you do this in class. Students who are good artists may enjoy drawing pictures to demonstrate some of the words. You may also be able to find ready-made pictures on the Internet.

2. Pronounce each word for your student, and point to the picture that shows what it means.

3. Write the words on the board, and ask your student to match a picture with each word.

4. Talk about the four seasons. Use the words in the lesson to describe and compare the seasons in each of your native cities. (Your native city may not be the one in which you are now teaching. Tell about it anyway as a way of getting to know each other better.) If you wish, make two charts like the one in the site sample so you can each place the words in appropriate boxes for your city.

Figure 2. Site Sample From ESL Lounge

Place these seasonal words into the correct box below.				
Heat wave	Drought	Snow	Leaves	Sun cream
Lamb	Sledging	Rain	Blizzard	Umbrella
Ice	Blossom	Flowers	Beach	Coat
Halloween	Ice cream	Sunbathe	Easter	Skiing
Windsurfing	Frost	Gales	Snowman	Puddles
Chestnuts	Thunderstorm	Skating	Thaw	Tan

Spring	Summer
Autumn/Fall	Winter

5. Relate the words to your student's life.
   - Ask whether your student has ever done any of the activities represented in the vocabulary list, such as skating, wind surfing, skiing, sunbathing, or sledging (sledding). Ask which ones the student likes best.
   - Have the student talk about his or her favorite season.
   - Ask whether the student has ever been in a gale or a blizzard.
6. Discuss the customs of Halloween and Easter, which may not exist in the student's native culture.
7. Have the student use the words relating to one season to write a short paragraph. (See the site sample below from Pearson Adult Learning Centre.)

You can use this type of lesson to teach both language and culture and to become better acquainted with your student's interests.

✦ Pearson Adult Learning Centre's *English Resources*
(http://palc.sd40.bc.ca/palc/resource.htm)

Target Audience

learners over 19 of all levels who want to learn or sharpen their English skills or pass the General Educational Development test

Special Features

- offers quizzes and worksheets in grammar, vocabulary, and writing
  — Grammar lessons are incorporated into writing lessons.
  — Writing lessons at lower levels may include a Teacher Sample to use as a model.
- specializes in self-paced learning
- integrates the Internet with students' studies
- provides links to practice questions for the Test of English as a Foreign Language (TOEFL), Graduate Management Admission Test (GMAT), and SAT
- provides an online reference for quick answers to grammar questions for all levels
- provides links to resources that include the following:
  — *Encyclopaedia Britannica*
  — library catalogues
  — job resources page
  — math tips archive
  — study skills pages

Site Sample: Basic Composition (Intermediate Level)

To use the site sample shown in Figure 3 for activities in a lesson, follow these steps:

1. Explain the three parts of a good paragraph: (a) the topic sentence (which tells what the paragraph is about), (b) the body (at least three sentences that explain and support the topic sentence), and (c) the conclusion (which summarizes or restates the topic sentence).

2. Find and label the three parts of a paragraph in the sample from the Teacher Writing Page.

3. Find the six adjectives in the sample. Discuss what they mean, and point out that *blue* can name a color or describe a feeling of sadness and that *funny* can mean *humorous* or *odd*. Ask which meanings apply to the paragraph.

4. Help the student list some topics with which the six adjectives in the assignment could be used (e.g., what the student usually does on a rainy day, a memorable rainy day from the past, a day the student hoped would not be rainy). Choose the best topic. If the student has trouble with the adjective choices, suggest others that would be easier to use.

Figure 3. Site Sample From **Pearson Adult Learning Centre**

Directions:
Write a short paragraph using all the adjectives. Be sure to write a good topic sentence, indent five spaces, and double space.

cozy	blue	funny
fuzzy	miserable	rainy

Teacher Writing Page

Winter Misery

The weather we have been having lately has made my life *miserable*. As a dog owner, I must walk outside every day, and, no matter what the weather, I spend between one and one and a half hours outside. The *rainy* conditions make me feel *blue*. My dog has even stopped asking, sometimes, to go outside for a walk. Lucky for me she often prefers her *cozy* perch on the end of my bed! Usually, however, we have to go out to give her some exercise. The park we go to is horrible these days: the rain has soaked the grass so much that ducks are swimming on the playing fields. That may seem *funny* to you, but when my old boots developed a leak this week I didn't think so. The cold water seeped all over my socks and I felt like I was walking barefoot through the park. I do love my dog very much, but this winter I would have preferred to put on my old *fuzzy* housecoat and sit, quietly reading my paper, watching the rain hurl itself against the windows of my house. This winter *misery* will end soon, I hope!

5. Help the student write a good topic sentence, and then have the student write the body and conclusion.

See also *Tips for Writers* (Pearson Adult Learning Centre, 2002c), which contains archived tips for writers of all levels.

When teaching writing, find some interesting content first, and then work on grammar and spelling problems. Getting ideas to write about is one of the most difficult things for students to do. A graphic organizer (see chapter 9) might help with the organization of ideas.

What Are Some Good Sites for Tutors of K–12 ESL Learners?

✦ *abcteach* (http://abcteach.com)

Target Audience

preschool and elementary school students (with some activities for middle and high school students)

Special Features

- "Basics" contains, for example, sections on alphabet activities, reading, reading comprehension, math, writing, handwriting (in manuscript and cursive), colors, and shapes.
- "Reading Comprehension" contains readings followed by comprehension questions for fictional and informational reading skills practice.
- "Theme Units" contains activities on, for example, animals, habitats, holidays, sports, countries, and states.
- "Fun Activities" includes crossword puzzles, number puzzles, online crosswords, word searches, unscrambles, and printable games.

Site Sample: Reading/Writing (Intermediate Level)

Use the site sample shown in Figure 4 after your student has read a book. Follow these steps:

1. On your dry-erase board, list all the main characters in the book.
2. Ask the student to choose two characters.
3. With your student, fill out a chart like the one in Figure 4 for one of the characters.
4. Ask the student to fill out another chart on the second character.
5. Help the student use the information from the chart to write a paragraph about one of the characters. The topic could be a description of the character's appearance and personality, the character's importance to the story, or qualities the student liked and did not like about the character.

✦ *Dave's ESL Café* (http://www.eslcafe.com)

Target Audience

all ages and levels

Special Features

- meanings and examples of phrasal verbs, slang expressions, and idioms
- "Pronunciation Power"

Figure 4. Site Sample From abcteach

Main Characters

Title of Book _____

Author _____

Fictional books always have main characters. Describe one main character in this book in detail. How did he/she look, what age was he/she, what was his/her personality like, etc.

Name of Character _____

Describe the character.

What was the importance of this character to the story?

Think about yourself. Fill out the form below and compare yourself to this character.

Alike	Not Alike

Did you like this character? Why or why not?

- quizzes in geography, grammar, history, idioms, words, slang, people, reading comprehension, science, world culture, and writing
- "Dave's Idea Cookbook," with ideas on how to teach math, music, reading, speaking, vocabulary, writing, spelling, grammar, listening, and other areas of ESL; and tips for tutors, many from ESL teachers in schools all over the United States and abroad

Site Sample: Phrasal Verb (Any Level)

To use the site sample shown in Figure 5 for activities in a lesson, follow these steps:

1. Explain to your student what a phrasal verb is: a verb phrase consisting of a verb plus a preposition. Sometimes a phrasal verb has an object, and sometimes it does not.

Sometimes the two words of the verb can be separated by the object, and sometimes they cannot.

2. Discuss reasons why one might say that the hay *burned up* but the barn *burned down* (e.g., *The fire "ate up" or consumed the hay; the barn fell down when it burned.*). You might tell your student that *be burned up* may also mean *be angry* (e.g., *I was really burned up when I locked my keys in the car*).

3. Work with your student to think of other sentences using *burn up* and *burn down*. Provide a list of objects like the following and decide whether they would *burn up* or *burn down*: a tree, a car, a cigarette, a house, firewood.

4. Discuss one or two other examples of phrasal verbs, such as *break up* and *break down*.

5. Present one phrasal verb each day in class. (*Dave's ESL Café* includes many more examples like the one shown in Figure 5.)

6. Have your student keep a notebook of phrasal verbs as you cover them in class.

7. Review one phrasal verb and teach one as a warmup activity in each lesson.

✦ *everythingESL* (http://www.everythingesl.net)

Target Audience

pre-K–12 students

Special Features

- advice on meeting the challenge of content instruction
- ways of organizing and assessing in the content area class
- tips on communicating
- ways to develop questioning strategies
- information on second language acquisition

Figure 5. Site Sample From Dave's ESL Café

---

burn up (usually no object): become destroyed/consumed by fire

Note 1: For people and small, non-stationary, non-upright things only

"All of Mr. Kennedy's hay burned up when his barn burned down."

Note 2: This phrasal verb is normally used without an object; when there is an object, the phrasal verb is separable.

"If you're looking for that old red shirt, you won't find it. I burned it up."

- content lessons on, for example,
  — "Categorizing and Classifying Animals"
  — "What's the Weather Like Today?"
  — "Amazing Animals"
- word searches and word puzzles
- links to off-site resources

Site Sample: Science Lesson on Amazing Animals (K–1; Beginning-Level ESL)

To use the site sample in Figure 6 for activities in a lesson, follow these steps:

1. Find pictures of animals. Select the ones you wish to teach your student.
2. Follow the guidelines given in the instructional sequence in the site sample. You and your student may want to make flash cards with the name of an animal on one side and a picture of the animal on the other as an aid to learning the animal names. (See chapter 9 for ways to use flash cards.)
3. Teach classification of information by choosing several animal habitats, such as *ocean, desert, pond,* and *forest*. Write or paste the name and picture of each habitat on a separate envelope. Ask the student to put each animal flash card in one of the habitat envelopes. (This activity is a *total physical response* [TPR] activity, in which the student responds by doing rather than speaking.)
4. Choose a short story about an animal. Make sure it has a lot of pictures and is written in easy English. If you do not have a suitable one at home, look for one on the Internet or at a public library. Read the story to your student.
5. Print duplicates of animal flash cards from an Internet site, and play a game of Go Fish. (See *ESL Flashcards*, n.d., for monkey, gorilla, bear, and animal habitat cards.)

✦ *English Club* (http://www.englishclub.com)

Target Audience

child–adult, high beginning–advanced level

Special Features

- lessons and activities for all language skills: grammar, pronunciation, vocabulary, listening, speaking, reading and writing
- sections on "Kids," "Games," and "Quizzes"
- language holidays
- ESL resources
- Web guide
- teacher education

Figure 6. Site Sample From everything ESL

Content Concepts and Skills
Animal vocabulary and habitats

Vocabulary Needed
Names of the most common zoo and farm animals; jungle; walk, run, swim, fly, crawl, hop, and climb

Materials or Resources
Pictures of animals from different classes; pictures of animal body parts and skin coverings; books with pictures of animals

Instructional Sequence for K–1 students and beginners in all grades
1. Teach the vocabulary for animal names.
2. Teach students to sort and classify information
3. Give students a variety of experiences with animals by reading books to them on different animals.
4. Once students have learned the names of various animals, have them categorize animals in different ways (how they move, where they live, what they eat, etc.)
5. Have students use charts and diagrams to compare animals in different ways.

Is It an Amphibian?

Name of Animal	Does it live on land and in the water?	Is it cold-blooded?	Are babies hatched from eggs?	Does it breathe air with lungs?	Does it have a backbone?	Is it an amphibian?
Frog						
Alligator						
Snake						
Toad						
Salamander						

Site Sample: Pronunciation (High Beginning Level or Above)

To use the site sample shown in Figure 7 for activities in a lesson, follow these steps:

1. Make four columns on your dry-erase board. At the top of each column, write one of the four words that shows one of the sounds a final *-∂* can make.

2. Say each word for your student, and ask the student to repeat it after you. Point out that when you add *-e∂* to a word that ends with *-t* or *-∂*, you also add another syllable to the word. For example, *want* has one syllable, but *wante∂* has two syllables.

3. Give your student a copy of the words and paragraph in the site sample. Say each word in the list of 20 words with a final [d] sound. Ask your student to tell or show

Figure 7. Site Sample from **English Club**

Pronunciation -ed

work > worked [t]   want > wanted [_d]
warn > warned [d]   weld > welded [_d]

1. landed		11. added
2. expected		12. wished
3. asked		13. liked
4. regarded		14. divided
5. decided		15. played
6. packed		16. multiplied
7. locked		17. listened
8. answered		18. listed
9. stopped		19. permitted
10. requested		20. explored

Reading Practice

When Bond arrived at the renovated Chateau, darkness had descended. He examined the shadowy building. Its ground-floor windows were closed and shuttered. He glanced at his watch. He concluded that there was no time to lose and decided to enter conventionally. He tried the gold-leafed front door but it was locked, barred and bolted. He realized he needed a ladder. He looked around and noticed one on the grass. Noiselessly, he propped it up against the freshly painted balcony and started to climb. He had nearly reached the top when he spotted headlights approaching. A large car pulled through the gate. By the time it arrived at the door, Bond had already jumped through the balcony window and discovered the cause of his anxiety.

you which of the 4 words on your board makes the same final [d] sound. For example, *landed* has the same final [ɪd] sound of *welded*.

4. Say each word again, and ask your student to repeat after you.

5. Read the paragraph to your student. Ask the student to underline the words that end with *-∂* as you read and to help you put each of these words in one of the four columns on the dry-erase board.

6. Read each sentence in the paragraph again. Ask your student to repeat each sentence after you. Ask your student to read the entire paragraph aloud. When the student feels comfortable with the pronunciation, have the student read the paragraph again as you record it on audiotape. Play back the recording. Ask the student to stop the recording if he or she hears a mistake. Do not stop the audiotape if the student misses a mistake. Just underline the mistakes on your copy of the reading as the audiotape continues.

7. Say and have the student repeat the individual words that were missed. Then have the student read each word in its sentence. Record again as the student reads the entire paragraph.

8. Praise the student for any improvement. Ask the student to practice reading the vocabulary list and paragraph aloud at home.

> Before using any lesson, activity, or exercise, preview it to be sure you know how to explain it to your student and to determine if it is at the right level for your student. Because Web sites are not heavily edited, you may also need to look for misspellings and grammatical inconsistencies.

Case Studies: Points of Interest

✦ Case Study 1
- Ms. Freeman finds vocabulary and pictures for her lesson on numbers and body parts on the Internet. Copying these materials on her printer saves much valuable time in preparing a lesson for the four Somali women.

✦ Case Study 2
- Ms. Hawkins plans to search on the Internet for materials to help Omar with his pronunciation of final consonants. Because Omar says he likes to be active, she will let him do some interactive exercises.

✦ Case Study 3
- Ms. Rogers plans to look on the Internet for some short, supplementary readings related to nursing and business. She wants to be sure Kim Su can say the words she will need while working as a nurse and when attending social functions related to her husband's business.

Observe and Reflect

1. Use the information from this chapter and from Appendix A to find an online number game that Ms. Freeman could use in her next class to reinforce numbers 1–50.

2. Look for an online pronunciation activity for Ms. Hawkins to help Omar with placing stress on the correct syllable in three- and four-syllable words.

3. Find an online grammar exercise that Ms. Rogers could use to help Kim Su with the final -s sound on plural nouns.

4. Find some online reference books you could use for your own tutoring. For example, do a search for an online ESL grammar or writing text.

CHAPTER 9

"How do I construct lessons for people whose language I do not speak?"

Use visual aids.

The first concern of many potential tutors of international students is how they can communicate with, let alone teach, a person who speaks another language. Two adages answer this problem: (a) A picture is worth a thousand words, and (b) actions speak louder than words. In other words, nothing breaks down communication barriers as well as visual aids. When displaying actual objects (i.e., realia) is impractical or the objects are unavailable, use pictures, graphs, charts, and gestures to present and clarify lessons at all levels. The use of visual aids is stimulating, attracts and holds your student's interest, and adds a creative dimension to your tutoring.

How Can I Use Visuals for Different Levels?

Visuals help beginning-level students understand the action indicated by certain verbs as they not only see but also imitate the action. In total physical response (TPR) activities, you demonstrate actions (e.g., opening and closing the door, standing up, walking toward a window) and then ask the student to imitate these actions. Pictures, too, are invaluable to beginning-level students, who make a direct association with words and objects without having to translate.

Intermediate-level students often rely on gestures and picture cues to understand verbal and written texts. Also, graphs, charts, and picture stories become cues for reading or oral responses.

Advanced students may benefit greatly from the opportunity to practice explaining pictures, graphs, and charts orally during lessons because this type of activity is common in the classroom, in the workplace, and on language proficiency tests, such as the Test of Spoken English (TSE©, published by Educational Testing Service; see Appendix B).

How Can I Use Pictures in Lesson Plans?

Almost all ESL texts use pictures to introduce or illustrate lessons. An appropriate picture lets students know what the lesson is about even if they cannot explain the image in English. In fact, a picture can be used to teach many content areas (e.g., math, social studies, history, science) or any of the four basic language skills (i.e., reading, writing, listening, and speaking). Picture dictionaries, especially those designed for ESL, are the easiest source of pictures on the many topics you may need for your students.

Suppose you want to teach a grammar/ conversation lesson on traditions in the U.S. family. First, present a picture like the one in Figure 1. Then prepare a lesson appropriate for your student's age and level. Below are some examples.

Figure 1. Picture for Lesson on U.S. Family Traditions

> Pictures like the one in Figure 1 are available from clipart collections, which you can find on the Internet or as part of some software programs, and from ESL Web sites (see Appendix A).

◆ Low Beginning Level

Low-beginning-level students might not know the words for members of a family or may recognize the words when they hear or see them but be unable to produce them orally. Here are some activities to accommodate such students.

* Write the words *mother/father, husband/ wife, son/ daughter,* and *brother/sister* on

your dry-erase board. If you want, give names to the members of the family in the picture.

- Ask your student *who* questions. Tell the student to point to the correct person in response. For example, you might ask, "Who is the mother?" or "Who is the father?" If the student is ready to speak, model the following question and answer: "Who is the son?" "The son is Tom White." Then repeat the question, "Who is the son?", and ask the student to give the answer.

- Ask the student to select magnetized labels referring to names of family members (e.g., sister, brother) and place each label next to the correct image in the picture.

> When beginning a new activity with a student, always demonstrate it by doing one example yourself first.

✦ High Beginning Level

A high-beginning-level student can produce short responses orally and answer questions like those in the following examples:

- Elicit information about the picture by asking, "What is the father doing?"

- Introduce new vocabulary, such as *lap* and *gift*, and ask, "What does Mrs. White have in her hand?"

- Use the picture to talk about certain verbs, such as *stand, wave, smile,* and *hide* . Write these verbs on the board, and ask the student to use them to tell a story about the picture.

> Do not correct every mistake. Just listen; if you understand the story, the student has communicated successfully. If you get the main idea but need clarification, model what you think the student said or meant.

✦ Low Intermediate Level

A low-intermediate-level student may benefit from looking at and discussing a picture before doing a reading or listening/speaking activity.

- Show the picture before doing a reading about U.S. families. Ask the student to tell you what the article is about from looking at the picture. Draw the student's attention to the title above the picture. Ask what kind of celebration the picture illustrates. Ask the student to tell you about a similar celebration in the student's native culture.

- If you are doing a listening/speaking lesson, ask the student to tell you what the people in the picture are saying to each other. Then write down the dialogue and act it out together.

When you use this type of introductory activity, you are using what the students already know to help them grasp new material (e.g., vocabulary, grammar, information).

✦ High Intermediate Level

For a high-intermediate-level student, bring in several photographs of families (including grandparents, aunts and uncles, and other family members) who are engaged in various activities, such as playing a game, eating a meal, working on a project, or celebrating a holiday.

1. Before the lesson, ask the student to bring in pictures of his or her own family.
2. Discuss the roles of each member of the family in the student's culture.
3. Write the words *mother, father, brother, sister, grandmother,* and *grandfather* across the board. Label one row *United States* and the other with the name of the student's culture (see Figure 2).
4. Write one or two words that come to mind about each family member.
5. Briefly discuss the role of each member in the student's native culture and in the United States.
6. Write this information on the chart. Point out and discuss similarities and differences between the two cultures.
7. Have the student write a paragraph or essay comparing the roles of family members in the two cultures.

✦ Advanced Level

The advanced-level student may need help with speaking skills in academic or professional settings.

• Ask the student to examine the picture for a minute to collect his or her thoughts, and then audio record the student describing the people and events portrayed.
• Look for a series of pictures, such as a comic strip, that tell a story. The TSE© generally shows four to six pictures with these instructions: "Tell me the story that the pictures

Figure 2. Chart Comparing Family Members' Roles

	Mother	Father	Brother	Sister	Grand-mother	Grand-father
United States						
China						

show in 60 seconds." The student preparing for this test can practice using pictures to tell stories in the tutoring sessions.

- Show the student how to use sequence words such as *first, then, next,* and *finally* to give a story cohesion and continuity. Let the student practice using a watch with a second hand to learn pacing.

> You do not always have to use photographs, clip art, or pictures from magazines. Even nonartists--like us--can draw a simple stick figure to illustrate almost any action or object (see the tips on drawing stick figures in this chapter).

How Can I Use Charts, Graphs, Maps, and Other Graphic Organizers in Lesson Plans?

Graphic organizers are helpful to students because they break down information from oral and written materials into comprehensible chunks. Once students understand the big picture, they can more easily digest details and new information.

You will probably not want to use graphs and charts with low-beginning-level students. However, these organizers can be used to introduce a content lesson or to teach reading, writing, grammar, or speaking to students of all other levels.

✦ Charts

The picture of the family shown in Figure 1 could be used to create a chart (see Figure 3) to show information about the members of the family and to teach grammar. After filling in the chart, do the following activities:

1. Teach a lesson on comparisons (e.g., *Tom is older than Susan. Mrs. White is older than Tom. Mr. White is the oldest of all. Tom likes pizza, and so does Susan.*).
2. Have the students make similar charts about their own family.
3. Ask the students to write sentences comparing the members of their family.

Figure 3. Chart for Comparing Family Members

	Mr. White	Mrs. White	Tom White	Susan White
Age	35	30	10	6
Height	6'2"	5'7"	5'5"	5"
Hobby	golf	gardening	video games	horseback riding
Favorite food	steak	pasta	pizza	pizza

> The student may need help finding English words for the items in the "favorite food" column of the chart, which may include foods from the student's native country.

Figure 4 shows another simple chart, similar to those used in ESL texts. To use such a chart with a student,

1. Make two copies of the chart.
2. Ask the student to fill in the last column of the chart with information about the city where the student came from or currently resides.
3. Compare that city with the others in the chart.
4. Help the student use the information to write a paragraph about the differences between the student's city and the other three cities.
5. Make an audiotape of the student explaining the information on the chart. Use the audiotape to work on the student's speaking skills.
6. Use the student's paragraph about the chart as the basis of a dictation or a cloze (see chapter 4 for samples).

Another type of chart, sometimes used in the TSE©, is an itinerary with changes written in (see Figure 5). The student must tell an audience about changes in the itinerary but must not simply read the printed information verbatim. This very advanced activity forces the student to use synonyms for the words on the schedule, create sentences in the future and present perfect tenses, and speak cohesively on audiotape--all in 90 seconds. To help your student read such a chart, make one like the one in Figure 5, substituting information about your own city. Then do the following activities:

1. Tell the student to cover all the topics in the chart but not all the details.
2. Give the student phrases to use (e.g., *instead of,* as in *We will do [X] instead of [Y]*).

Figure 4. City Comparison Chart

Season of Year: Winter				
	City			
	Chicago	Seattle	Miami	Student's city
Weather	cold, windy snow, ice	cool, mild rain	warm, mild humidity	
Things to do	go to the theater	go for a walk	go to the beach	
Sports	ice skating	hiking	water skiing	

Figure 5. Sample Itinerary

SIGHTS OF MEMPHIS TOURS
4016 Poplar Ave.
Memphis, TN

Date:	Monday, July 5	
Transportation:	Luxury Limousine, Inc.	*change to chartered bus*
Depart:	9 a.m.—Sights of Memphis Tours parking lot	
Itinerary:	9:45 a.m.—Graceland	*change time to 10 a.m.*
	12:00 a.m.—Picnic lunch at the Memphis Botanical Gardens	
	2:00 p.m.—Pink Palace Museum	*change to Civil Rights Museum (Pink Palace is closed for repairs)*
	4:00 p.m.—Mudd Island	
	6:30 p.m.—Dinner at the Rendezvous	
Return:	9:30 p.m. (approximately)	
Cost:	$25 (excluding admission and dinner)	*change: dinner included due to cancellation of limousine*

3. Teach synonyms or word forms that will help the student avoid reading the information (e.g., *return* for *We will come back, date* for *time, transportation* for *We will travel by, depart* for *departure time, itinerary* for *We will go to*).

4. Tell the student to play the role of the tour director who does not want the tourists to be disappointed about the changes. Model what the tour guide might say if your student has difficulty. Point out when to use present, past, and future tenses. Here is one model:

    Please take out your schedule for our upcoming sightseeing trip and note four changes. We will leave on Monday, July 5, but we will use a chartered bus instead of a limousine. The departure time and place will remain the same. There are two itinerary changes: We'll be at Graceland at 10:00 a.m. instead of 9:45. At 2:00 p.m. we'll go to the Civil Rights Museum instead of the Pink Palace, which is closed for repairs. The rest of the itinerary remains the same. We still plan to return by 9:30 p.m. Here's the good news: $25 now includes dinner because of the cancellation of the limousine.

✦ Graphs

Some texts present the student with graphs on various topics. The student must listen to information on an audiotape to fill in the graph. If you do not have a textbook, you can find many graphs appropriate for students of different levels in magazines such as *Reader's Digest* and newspapers such as *USA Today.* You can use the reproducible Temperature Graph at the end of this chapter to create your own graph by keeping track of the temperature over a period of time in one or more cities.

An advanced-level student may need practice explaining a graph to an audience of classmates or fellow professionals or for an English proficiency test such as the TSE©. Create the framework for a graph (see Figure 6), and ask the student to research the missing information.

After the student has filled in the information in the graph, ask questions about the graph and give the student a specific amount of time in which to answer:

Explain the information given in the graph. (60 seconds)

What future trend does the graph indicate? (45 seconds)

To help your student read a graph,

1. Tell the student to use the title and words on the chart.

2. Provide a framework and phrases the student can use to explain the graph, for example,

This graph explains _____. [Use the title of the graph.] In the year _____, the average American man lived _____ years. From the year _____ to _____ the average life expectancy for males [increased/decreased] from _____ to _____. From this graph we can see that male life expectancy rates have [risen/fallen/fluctuated] [little/somewhat/greatly] in the past century and will probably _____ in the future.

3. Change the information in the chart to show, for example, unemployment rates in the United States from 1900 to 2000. Ask the student to explain changes in the chart and phrase framework.

Figure 6. Sample Graph

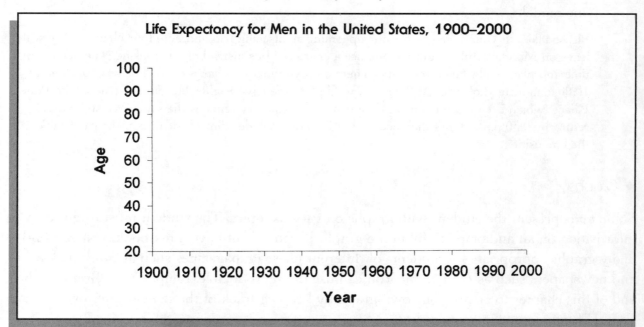

✦ Maps

Your students may also benefit from practice in looking at a map and giving directions, another activity commonly found on the TSE©. Using a map of a local college or university campus,

1. Circle two locations in red. Label one location *Point A* and the other *Point B.*

2. If necessary, demonstrate how to give directions by choosing two other locations on the map and giving directions from one to the other. Your student may need assistance with such vocabulary as *north, south, east, west, right,* and *left*

3. Ask your student to look at the map and tell you how to get from Point A to Point B.

For practice in receiving directions, audio record the directions from a specified place on the map to an unlabeled place. Have the student listen to the audiotape, follow the directions, and label the unmarked place correctly.

✦ Graphic Organizers

A graphic organizer is a visual aid that helps students organize and simplify specific types of information in a meaningful way. For example, you could use a graphic organizer to help your student gather important information from a reading passage or organize ideas for a paragraph about a passage (see the Reading/Writing Diagram included as a reproducible form at the end of this chapter).

Figures 7 and 8 show two different ways to organize the same information gathered from a reading passage. The diagram shown in Figure 9, based on the following simplified version of

Figure 7. Graphic Organizer for a Story

Title Name of book/story	
Author Who wrote the story?	
Main characters Name Relation to others Physical description Character/personality	
Setting Time Place	
Theme What did you learn from the story?	

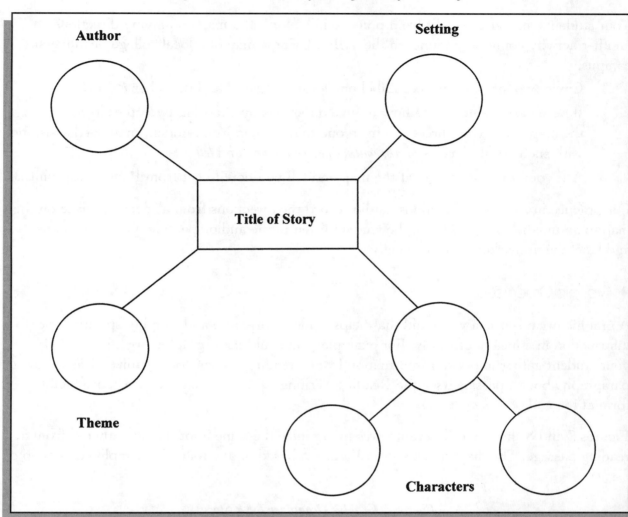

Figure 8. Alternate Graphic Organizer for a Story

Author

Setting

Title of Story

Theme

Characters

"Our Changing Lifestyles: Trends and Fads" (Kirn & Hartmann, 1990, pp. 74–75), is yet another way to organize information from a reading passage. (See also the reproducible Spider Map and Information Organizer at the end of this chapter.)

> The lifestyles of people in the United States change very quickly. It's not just their clothes and hairstyles that change; everything they do, from their food preferences to exercise habits, is subject to change. One year men and women wear blue jeans and boots and keep sunglasses on top of their heads. Fashionable people are eating sushi in Japanese restaurants and drinking white wine. Parents are naming their children "Heather," "Dawn," or "Eric." The next year women are wearing long skirts, people are drinking bottled water from France, and parents are naming their children "Tiffany," or "Jason." Even people can be "in" or "out." In 1981 Americans were quoting the three words of an elderly woman in a television commercial who loudly asked, "Where's the beef?" Americans also like to follow the lives of sports heroes and politicians who are popular and successful at the moment. What causes these fads to come and go? The desire to make money may cause designers and advertisers to promote new fashions. But money is not the only factor. Teenagers often create their own slang words such as "groovy," "awesome," or "rad" instead of saying "wonderful" because they want to be part

of something new and creative and be part of an "in group." You could say that many Americans feel there is something wrong if there is not frequent change in their lives. (From E. Kirn and P. Hartmann, *Interactions II: A reading skills book*, 1990, New York: McGraw-Hill. Copyright 1990 The McGraw-Hill Companies. Reprinted with permission of The McGraw-Hill Companies.)

Use the graphic organizer that works best for your student. You can design your own or do a search on the Internet (see Appendix A) for a variety of organizers for different purposes.

How Can I Use Signs and Symbols in Lessons?

U.S. communities are full of signs that send important messages. Familiarize your students with traffic signs for cars and pedestrians (see Figure 10 for examples) as well as labels that warn consumers that the contents are highly toxic. Canned and packaged foods may also

Figure 9. Diagram Based on "Our Changing Lifestyles: Trends and Fads"
(Kirn & Hartmann, 1990, p. 74–75)

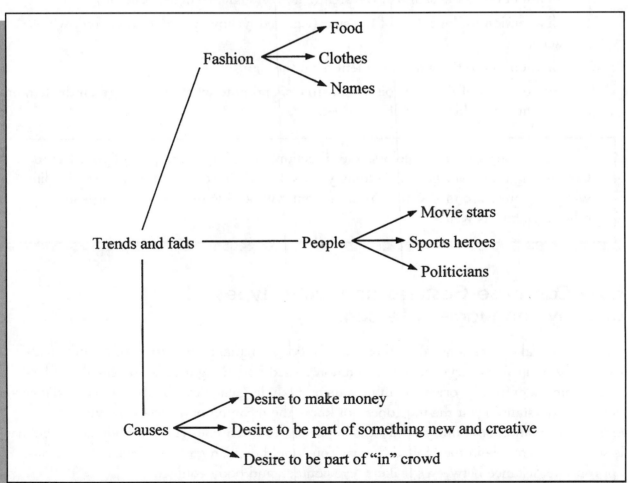

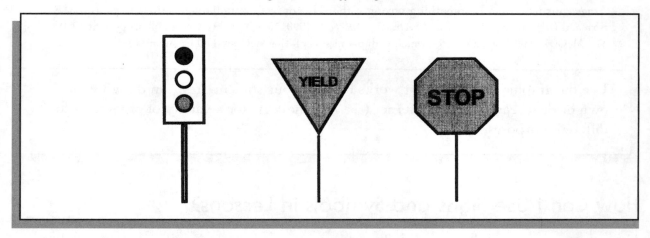

Figure 10. Traffic Signs

contain visual signs of their contents that will help non-English speakers know what to buy. Gather some household products that bear these important visual aids, and teach your student some practical lessons.

To help your student read signs,

1. Call attention to the shape of the sign (e.g., rectangle, triangle, octagon).
2. Call attention to the colors of the sign (e.g., red, yellow, green, orange, red, white, black).
3. Call attention to the words and letters on the sign.
4. Show pictures of the signs on actual streets, and note whether they are on the left, on the right, or in the center of the street.

> The vocabulary of shapes, colors, and directions is an important part of your lesson. Connecting these words to something your student will see and use in every day life will give your lesson relevance. Your student will be able to use these words in other contexts as well.

How Can I Use Gestures and Other Types of Body Language in Lessons?

Gestures, facial expressions, and other types of body language are a form of communication used daily by nearly everyone. Some commonly used body language is universally understood; some is culturally oriented. In fact, using body language can be the source of dangerous misunderstandings if the user does not know the meaning of a certain gesture or expression in another country. Thus it is important to teach your student body language that is socially acceptable in the United States. You should explain gestures, facial expressions, appropriate distance between speakers, eye contact, and body contact.

✦ Gestures and Facial Expressions

- Use a gesture for each of the following expressions, and ask your student what each means: *Good luck; Hello; Good-bye; Be quiet; You mean me?; I'm shocked!; I don't understand.*

- Ask your student to explain the hand gestures and facial expressions shown in Figure 11.

- Discuss gestures that have a different meaning in your student's native country than they do in the United States.

- Discuss and compare rude and acceptable gestures in both countries.

- Teach your beginning-level students the following instructional gestures:

  — Cupping your ear with your hand means *listen.*

  — Using a summoning gesture with your hand means *speak.*

  — Holding up your hand in a halting motion means *be silent.*

You can create your own gestures to communicate many instructions.

Figure 11. Gestures and Facial Expressions

✦ Distance Between Speakers

The amount of acceptable distance between two speakers varies from culture to culture. Standing too far apart may indicate unfriendliness, hostility, or lack of interest. Standing too close together may indicate intimacy or intimidation. In the United States, normal conversational distance varies from 3 to 4 feet between those who are not well acquainted or who want to show respect for difference in rank and is about $1\frac{1}{2}$ feet between family members and friends. Address this issue with your students because the norms for distance between speakers may differ in their cultures.

✦ Eye Contact

Acceptable forms of eye contact also differ among cultures. Americans tend to think that someone who fails to look them directly in the eye during most of the conversation is untrustworthy or not paying attention. However, in some other cultures (e.g., some Asian cultures), looking directly at someone is considered rude or disrespectful. Observe your student to determine if you need to address this issue.

✦ Body Contact

Acceptable body contact also varies greatly around the world. In some European countries, men and women lightly kiss each other on both cheeks as a sign of friendship. Most Americans would probably prefer a handshake, although they might hug a very close friend regardless of sex. In Europe, two girls who are very good friends may walk hand-in-hand down the street, but in the United States only very young children might do so. Some Americans frequently touch the arm or shoulder of someone they are conversing with even when they do not know the person well. People from Europe may be more understanding of this informal behavior, but those from Asian cultures tend to be more reserved and formal.

To avoid embarrassing your student or creating a misunderstanding, you may want to check on appropriate body language in the student's culture. One readily available resource for information on this topic is *Letitia Baldrige's New Complete Guide to Executive Manners* (Baldrige, 1993), which is available in bookstores, libraries, and even some office supply stores. Other cultural reference texts are listed in Appendix A.

> Do not rely on a student's body language to indicate understanding. Students from some cultures nod and smile in response to everything you say out of respect for your role as their teacher. Obtain confirmation your student has grasped your message by getting the student to demonstrate mastery in an oral or written form.

How Can I Make My Own Visual Aids?

✦ Flash Cards

You can use flash cards to reinforce vocabulary; reteach a story, article, or textbook chapter; and develop reading skills.

To teach or reinforce vocabulary with beginning-level students, combine pictures and vocabulary to create flash cards. Simply draw or cut out a picture, and attach it to one side of a 3-in.-by-5-in. index card (see Figure 12 for an example). On the opposite side, write the corresponding English word. For example, you could put a facial expression on one side and the emotion it expresses on the other.

In tutoring high-beginning- and intermediate-level students in reading, you can use flash cards to identify important characters from a story or important people in history (see the example in Figure 12). Many students will have sufficient reading skills to recognize names even if they have difficulty pronouncing them. You might also put pictures of the explorers (obtained, e.g., from the Internet) next to their names. Along with similar flash cards showing places and events, such flash cards could be used for a lesson on important explorers of the New World.

Figure 12. Flash Cards

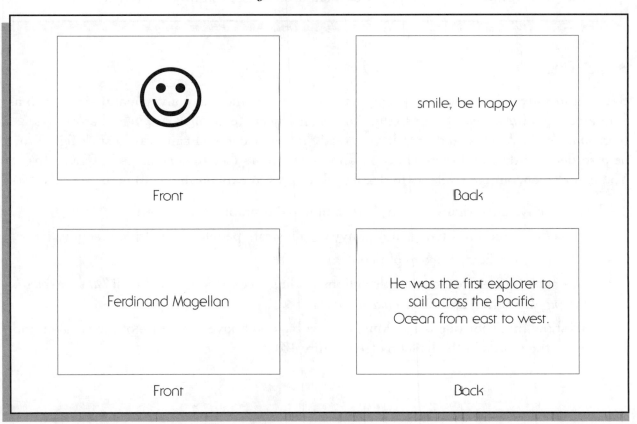

- Ask the student to place all the cards showing explorers from Spain, for example, in one pile, those from England in another pile, and so on.

- Use the flash cards to develop reading skills by showing the student an explorer's name on the front of a flash card. Show your student how to scan a page of text to find the explorer's name. Then ask the student to read the information about the explorer in the text.

- Put the flash cards in chronological order, and let the student use them to retell the story of the New World explorers.

- Give the student the information on the back of an explorer flash card along with the number of the page containing the name of the corresponding explorer. In this relatively advanced activity, the student must use key words on the flash card to find the person.

- For grade school or middle school students, make a game out of the flash cards. Give points for every person or event the students can identify on the first try. Let them keep the cards they have mastered on their side of the table while you keep the cards the students still need to work on. Repeat until the students have all the cards on their side of the table.

> In making flash cards for content areas like history, keep the grammar and vocabulary as simple as possible so the students have the opportunity to demonstrate their knowledge of history. Let them use the English they already know.

✦ Stick Figures

Stick figures are easy to draw, are simple to understand, and can convey many ideas, such as emotions (e.g., *happy, sad*), actions (e.g., *sit, stand*), objects (e.g., *table, chair*), and attributes (e.g., *tall, short*). When you do not have a ready-made visual, you can draw a stick figure to help students understand these concepts and many others (see the examples in Figure 13). You can also encourage students to draw stick figures to explain things to you.

To draw effective stick figures, keep them simple—the simpler, the better:
- Use circles and lines (straight or wavy) to illustrate people, animals, and actions.
- Use size to indicate the age of people.
- Use stick figures to show simple actions leading to questions, such as *What is he doing?*, *Do you play soccer?*, and *Do you like to play games?*
- To show that someone is speaking, draw a balloon above the figure of the speaker and write the words in the balloons (see Figure 13).

Figure 13. Stick Figures

Case Studies: Points of Interest

✦ Case Study 1

- Because the Somali women are at the beginning level, they have a great need for visual aids to help them understand the lesson. Ms. Freeman therefore uses pictures and gestures as visual aids to understanding body parts.

✦ Case Study 2

- Ms. Hawkins uses pictures in a reading passage to help Omar anticipate what he is going to read.
- She can use visuals in English and social studies to enhance Omar's reading comprehension.

✦ Case Study 3

- Ms. Rogers uses a scale to measure Kim Su's pronunciation skills and to build Kim Su's confidence in what she has already accomplished.
- She will require Kim Su to read graphs and charts in the pronunciation text *Well Said* (Grant, 2001).

All three tutors use at least one visual aid. Although the need for visual aids decreases at the higher levels, these three case studies clearly demonstrate how the tutor's use of visual aids can benefit students of any age, language level, or language goal.

Observe and Reflect

1. Create a lesson plan using the Lesson Planning Sheet at the end of chapter 7. Find or create some visual aids to support your lesson.

2. Make a list of common U.S. gestures you think your student should know.

3. Gather products from around your house that use signs or symbols to communicate contents, usage, or a warning (e.g., canned goods, cleaning products, and medicines).

4. Could any of the tutors in the case studies use a graphic organizer to help their students? Explain.

Temperature Graph

	Monday	Tuesday	Wednesday	Thursday	Friday	Saturday	Sunday
70° F							
60° F							
50° F							
40° F							
30° F							

Reading/Writing Diagram

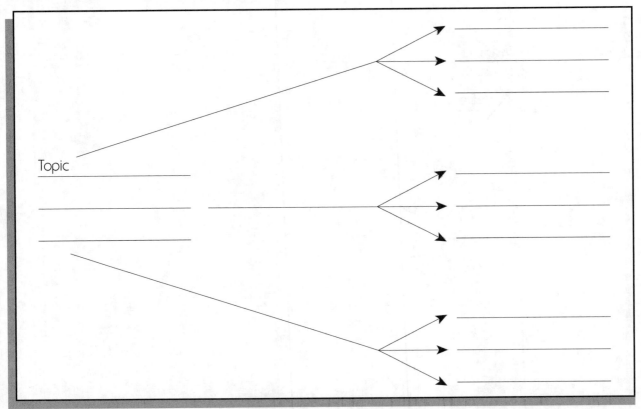

Topic _____

Spider Map

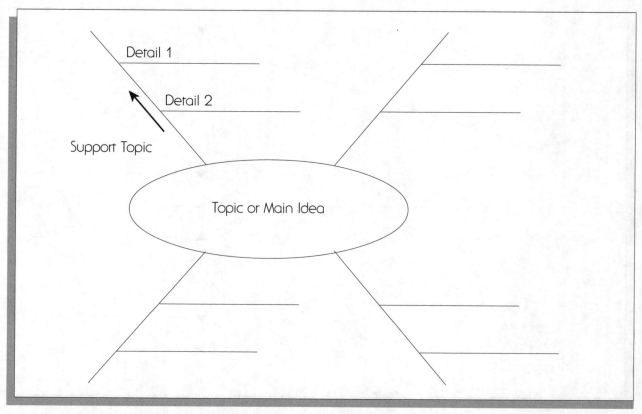

Detail 1

Detail 2

Support Topic

Topic or Main Idea

Information Organizer

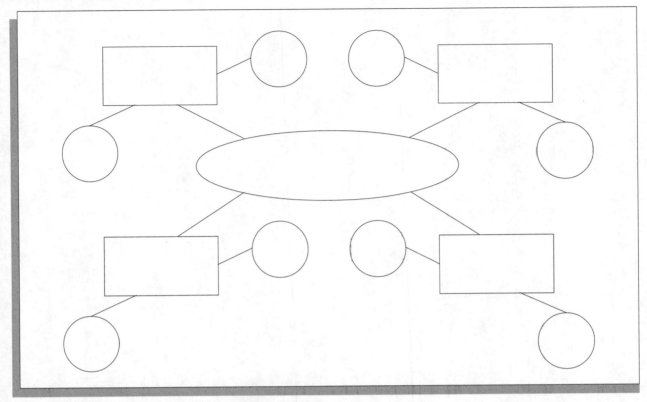

Unit 4: Evaluate

The last requirement of PACE is to evaluate the student and, by doing so, evaluate your tutoring. As you tutor, you want to know, "Am I effective? Has the student been learning?" Evaluation, a step often neglected by tutors, is necessary to ensure that your tutoring is helping students reach their goals. This unit will assist you in evaluating and documenting students' progress both formally and informally and in evaluating your own performance as an ESL tutor. It will also advise you on what to do when students do not progress as well as expected.

CHAPTER 10

"How do I document students' progress and evaluate their success?"

Use formal and informal means.

Evaluation has traditionally meant formal testing. Although testing is one way to evaluate, it is not the only way, and for your purposes it may not be the best way. The most effective teachers use a combination of formal and informal means of evaluation. *Formal* evaluation includes tests—teacher-made, provided with the teacher's edition of texts, and standardized. *Informal* evaluation includes such methods as portfolios, checklists, observations, interviews, self-evaluation charts, and journals. You should decide what to use based on your student's needs, age, and ability. Tutors generally use informal evaluation because it reveals the information the tutor needs: what and how much the student knows, not what the student does not know.

If you think of the process as *evaluating* instead of *testing*, you will actually be doing so each time you meet with the student. A test is a means of measuring something specific that you have taught; it measures outcomes. For example, you may want to know that the student has mastered one concept or skill before moving on to the next. Because learning a language is really developing a skill, you will want to evaluate—that is, measure progress in skill building—rather than just test, in a number of ways.

Some students may need help preparing for standardized tests, such as the General Educational Development test, the Test of English as a Foreign Language (TOEFL©), the Test of English for International Communication (TOEIC©), the Test of Spoken English (TSE©), the Graduate Management Admission Test (GMAT©), or the Graduate Record Examination (GRE©) (see chapters 7 and 9). You can use the practice tests provided in the preparation materials for these tests. After reviewing the format and content with the student, have the student take a practice test in a simulated testing situation, and use the results to determine what material the student must continue practicing.

What Are Some Means of Formal Evaluation?

Although you may not do any specific formal evaluation, you should be aware of formal testing formats in case you need to prepare students for tests they will take at school, to get a job or promotion, or to become U.S. citizens. Many formal tests include items in multiple-choice, true-false, or matching formats; each format has advantages and disadvantages, as shown in Table 1.

What Techniques Can I Use to Evaluate the Student While Tutoring?

Some teaching/tutoring techniques (e.g., total physical response [TPR], cloze, dictation, and short-answer activities) are also means of assessments (see Table 2). Students become familiar with these techniques and do not perceive them to be tests even when you use them for evaluation.

✦ Total Physical Response

For beginning-level students, you might use TPR activities for language practice because they allow learners to demonstrate their understanding of language without requiring much active use of language. For example, you can ask the student to look at a picture and point to the items you name. Or you might ask the student to give one-word responses to questions about pictures (e.g., "How many children are there?" "Is it a supermarket or a library?" "What do you see?"). You gear the TPR activity to the material the student has learned.

As means of assessment, TPR activities allow you to evaluate beginning-level learners who can recognize language forms but have no way of expressing their knowledge. Also, in testing language, TPR activities rely not on language but on visuals. You may adapt any pictures or drawings from texts, magazines, or picture books to the students' needs. The disadvantage of TPR activities as means of assessment is that students generally use no language skills of their own or produce only one- or two-word answers. TPR activities are, however, a good way to evaluate comprehension.

Table 1. Formal Test Types

Test Type	What It Tests	Appropriate Levels	Advantages	Disadvantages
Multiple choice	Knowledge of grammar items, reading comprehension, and content areas	All; reading ability required	Samples available on the Internet can test grammar points and vocabulary and help the student understand and prepare for the testing process.	Tests are difficult to construct; many international students are unaware of the format.
True/false or yes/no	Speaking or reading comprehension, content areas	All; especially good for lower levels	Test can be used with students from beginning to advanced levels.	Responses are limited to simple ones; students must analyze statements.
Matching	Reading comprehension, word recognition	Low intermediate–advanced	Tests are easy to grade and construct.	Students must have a good reading level; the items test passive knowledge only and allow guessing.

✦ Cloze Activities

Cloze, or fill-in-the-blank, activities are a way to evaluate intermediate- or advanced-level learners (see chapter 4). A cloze activity provides a fragment of a reading selection with items deleted; the student must add those items. You can use a cloze activity to evaluate specific knowledge by deleting vocabulary or grammatical items the students have studied. For example, you might delete all prepositions from a text. Once you have reviewed preposition usage, ask the students to fill in the blanks with a correct preposition. They see this as an application of what they have learned; you use it as a means of evaluation. You might also combine a cloze activity with a matching test by supplying a list of items from which the students must choose.

The advantage of the cloze is that it allows you to evaluate the student's language skills in longer discourse, not just isolated sentences, and the student can therefore demonstrate, for example, pronoun use and other reference features. In addition, you can construct your own cloze or make one from a text. The disadvantage of using cloze activities in evaluation is that you must decide whether to count as correct answers only those words or forms you

Table 2. Teaching Techniques Used as Assessments

Test Type	What It Tests	Appropriate Levels	Advantages	Disadvantages
Total physical response (TPR)	Comprehension	Beginning	Can be used to evaluate beginning-level learners who recognize language forms but cannot express their knowledge; uses visuals	Students generally use no language skills of their own or produce only one- or two-word answers.
Cloze activities	Grammar, vocabulary, content areas	Intermediate–advanced	Can be mixed with a matching test; tests skills in language discourse, not just isolated sentences; allows testing of, for example, pronoun use and other reference features	The tutor must decide how to score the test and interpret the final score.
Dictations	All skills, including writing conventions and spelling	Intermediate–advanced	Is easy to construct, especially if a reading selection from the textbook is used; is a means of determining how well students make associations between what they hear and how words are represented in writing; is easy to grade	The test relies on the student's ability to hear and understand; it should be used only with students who have writing and grammar skills at the intermediate level or above; the test might prove to be too difficult if the tutor does not select the passage well.
Short answer, short essay	Writing	Advanced	Allows advanced-level students to demonstrate language skill as well as knowledge; challenges students to use higher level thinking skills	Scoring relies on the tutor's judgment of the student's success.

anticipated or any acceptable words or forms. If you accept any form that is not strictly incorrect, you must make a judgment about correctness. Some tutors do not feel comfortable doing this and want a more objective means of evaluating.

✦ Dictation

Dictation (see chapter 4) is a technique that has stood the test of time. The teacher reads a passage, and the student writes it down. Teachers have their own preferred ways of giving dictation, but they usually read a passage at least twice, once at normal speed and once more slowly. To take dictation tests successfully, students must use listening, writing, and reading skills.

Students also display knowledge of writing conventions and spelling through dictation. They must listen carefully for specific words and make judgments about the use of *homophones*— words that sound alike but are spelled differently. You can combine dictation with a cloze activity by providing a text with blanks that the students must fill in as they listen. This combination is helpful in focusing students' listening on features that may be troublesome, such as final *-s* on present tense verbs, possessives, or plurals. Short dictations can be a part of every tutoring session.

An advantage of the dictation is that it is easy to construct, especially if you use part of a reading selection from a textbook. The dictation is a good means of determining how well the students can make associations between what they hear and how words are represented in writing. It is also easy to evaluate. The disadvantage of the dictation is that, because it relies on the student's ability to hear and understand, it might prove to be too difficult for some students if you do not select the passage carefully. For this reason, dictation should be used with students who have relatively advanced-level skills in writing and grammar.

✦ Short Answer or Short Essay

The short-answer activity or short essay requires students to use language to demonstrate an advanced-level skill. You might ask high intermediate– or advanced-level students to respond to questions on topics covered in the tutoring sessions. You would then evaluate their knowledge of the content and their ability to express their knowledge using English.

The advantages of the short-answer evaluation are that it provides a means for advanced-level students to demonstrate language skill as well as knowledge and challenges students to use higher level thinking skills. The disadvantage is that it relies on the tutor's judgment of how successful the student is compared with others at the same level when there is no peer group with which to compare results.

What Is Informal Evaluation?

If you prefer not to use tests, then you might use informal evaluation (e.g., observations, checklists, portfolios, self-evaluation charts, interviews, and journals) as a means of documenting students' progress.

✦ Teacher Observations

You can evaluate students through simple observation. Making observation notes should be your final activity for each lesson. The accumulated observations make up a progress report for the student.

You might decide to provide a progress report on a regular basis—every 4 weeks, for example. Looking at your observations, you will note whether the student has improved, continues to improve, or shows little or no improvement in the areas you have tracked. You then report to the student, parent, or sponsoring agency. The accumulated observation notes also tell whether your tutoring has been effective. If you see that the student has made no improvement, has not reached the short-term goals you have set, or seems to be backsliding, you will need to review your approaches and lessons plans.

✦ Checklists

Another way to evaluate progress is to keep a checklist of the student's achievements (see Figures 1 and 2; see also the reproducible Skill Checklist at the end of this chapter). When you first determine the student's needs, make a checklist based on the goals you want to reach, whether they relate to grammar, topics, communication, or content areas. On your checklist, break down the goals into parts so that you can note the date on which the student demonstrates ability in an area. You should also review from time to time to reinforce learning, and the checklist is a way of knowing what skills your have covered and when you did so.

For example, you may note that the student has demonstrated the ability to respond to questions about personal information (i.e., name, address, telephone number). Later, you may want to ask questions that elicit this information to ensure that the student has indeed mastered it. Or you may have noted on an observation form that your advanced-level student can read intermediate-level material for the main idea and checked off the item *reads for main idea* on your checklist. Two weeks later, you might have the student read a short passage and ask questions about the main points of the reading. If the student maintains the skill you are assessing, you might add a second date and check mark to the checklist.

✦ Portfolios

Portfolios have a variety of purposes—documenting progress from the beginning of the tutoring sessions to the end or showcasing the student's best, supposedly most representative, work. Both types of portfolios develop the student's skills of self-evaluation (see below).

Figure 1. Skill Checklist With Observation Notes for Beginning-Level Oral Skills

Student: *José Herrera*
Check (✔) and date as behavior is observed.

Observed skills	Date Sept. 1–Oct. 31	Date Nov. 1–Dec. 31	Date Jan. 1–Feb. 28
Responds to personal questions (e.g., name, address, telephone number)	✔ Sept. 7	✔ Nov. 5—expands information	✔ Feb. 1—provides information without much prompting
Asks personal questions of others	✔ Oct. 10 ✔ Oct. 29	✔ Nov. 20	✔ Jan. 18
Initiates conversation		✔ Nov. 3 ✔ Nov. 20	✔ Jan. 10
Identifies members of family and gives information about them		✔ Nov. 2 ✔ Dec. 6	
Uses numbers; identifies numbers used for money, time, and date	✔ Sept. 30 (numbers to 100; cardinal only); identifies coins and dollar bills	✔ Nov. 5 (uses and recognizes up to 1,000); can do simple arithmetic	✔ Feb. 7 (uses and recognizes both cardinal and ordinal numbers)
Names items present or in a picture	✔ Sept. 10 (items in the room)	✔ Oct. 9 (food items in a picture dictionary)	✔ Jan. 10 (items in a picture story; narrates simply)

Student portfolios (see Figure 3; see also the reproducible Portfolio for Tutoring Sessions at the end of the chapter) are a good way to involve students, parents, and sponsoring agencies in the role of evaluation. Portfolios may contain notes, computer-printed handouts, graphs, charts, rough drafts, audio- or videotapes of the student reading or engaging in conversation, journal entries, and other work samples. The portfolio helps students refresh their memory of tasks they have completed and allows them to see the progress they have made. Usually students can bring their portfolios to show their parents or sponsors.

✦ Self-Evaluation

Students may keep self-evaluation charts in which they record their achievements based on their own goals and description of their own abilities (see Figure 4 and the reproducible Self-Evaluation Chart at the end of the chapter). They track the skills they have mastered in the tutoring sessions, possibly dating each entry and commenting on their goals as they make progress.

Figure 2. Writing Skills Checklist

Skill	Date(s) observed
Capital letters ___at the beginning of a sentence ___for proper nouns and adjectives ___in titles of books, magazines, and other publications	
Spelling plural forms of nouns ___ regular nouns ___ nouns ending in -y preceded by a consonant (e.g., *party, family, city*) ___ nouns ending in -ss, -sh, -x, and -ch (e.g., *kiss, wish, box, watch*) ___ irregular nouns (e.g., *child/children, mouse/mice, foot/feet, leaf/leaves*)	
Spelling verb forms ___ -ed form of regular verbs ___ past form of irregular verbs ___ past participle of irregular verbs ___ -ing forms of all verbs ___ one-syllable verbs ending in one consonant preceded by one vowel ___ two-syllable verbs with stress on second syllable ending in one consonant	
Sentences ___ complete sentences ___ sentence variety (simple, compound, complex)	
Punctuation ___ comma ___ semicolon ___ quotation marks ___ period	
Paragraph ___ topic sentence ___ support information ___ conclusion ___ transitional devices	
Essay ___ introduction with thesis ___ supporting paragraphs ___ conclusion	

◆ Interviews

By interviewing students, you can ensure that they feel they are making progress. In the interview, ask your students to evaluate their skills and tell you in which areas they have improved, what techniques have worked, and in which areas they need further work.

Figure 3. Portfolio Contents for Tutoring Sessions on Emerging Writing Skills

Student: *Ming-li Zhao* Dates covered: *Sept. 3–Nov. 30*			
Entry	September	October	November
Samples of alphabet copied			
Samples of words and sentences copied			
Written samples of name and other personal information			
Sample dictations of words			
Audiotape of student reading words she has written			
Tutor checklist of observed behavior			
Samples of student writing: sentences or longer discourse			
Note. All items should be dated.			

Figure 4. Self-Evaluation Chart for Advanced-Level Student

Name: *Kim Su*	
What I want to learn	*What I have learned*
Improve pronunciation when speaking	*June 3: Ms. Rogers asked me to read some things and then told me what sounds I have difficulty with. I will work on those.* *June 10: I am doing better with the r and l sounds but still need work on th; intonation still needs work.* *July 10: The book is helping me know why I have difficulty. I know my problems and must practice.* *July 21: Ms. Rogers says my intonation is much better.*
Converse comfortably in social situations	*June 3: I can talk easily with Ms. Rogers but not others.* *June 21: I have used some things I learned and am trying to talk more to people at my work. I still don't always understand when they answer.* *July 10: Today I talked for several minutes with the cashier. I understood her and she understood me.*
Understand clients at work	*June 3: Ms. Rogers says some people speak English with accents. They come from different areas. I don't understand some people when they speak.* *June 15: I practiced first with people I understand in the lab like the doctors. Next I will try to talk to someone in the cafeteria.* *July 15: I talked with a patient today to explain medicine. She understood me and asked questions. I could answer.*

The interview itself gives students an opportunity to demonstrate language skill. You might wish to add the results of the interview to your observation notes on the skill checklist for that student.

✦ Journals

Reflective journals can help you evaluate tutoring sessions. Students who can write at the intermediate level can keep a journal of learning that highlights what was covered in each session, what they have learned, and what they still need to work on. You, too, might keep a journal that documents successes and failures.

You now have a variety of means to evaluate a student's success. Choose a means appropriate for the student and one you feel comfortable using.

Case Studies: Points of Interest

✦ Case Study 1

- Ms. Freeman uses a checklist to monitor the progress of her four Somali students.
- She uses informal testing to evaluate them and notes the date of her evaluation.
- She keeps an observation journal of their demonstrated skills and relies on TPR activities to test comprehension.
- After the first 8-week session, she gives an evaluation of each student to the sponsoring agency.

✦ Case Study 2

- Omar must pass his subject-matter courses at school and has some personal language goals that Ms. Hawkins will work on in the tutoring sessions.
- Ms. Hawkins will test Omar formally on the material he learns for school, check his understanding, and simulate the testing situation he will encounter in the classroom.
- She will use Omar's quiz and test scores at school to monitor his progress.
- She will use mostly informal means to evaluate the specific language problems she notes in her assessment. To evaluate speaking, she will use interviews, a portfolio of audiotapes, and observations. To evaluate reading, she will use a combination of formal and informal testing, using some formal tests suggested by Omar's teacher. Informal evaluation of reading will include keeping a checklist of reading skills and observations.

✦ Case Study 3

- Ms. Rogers uses her observations of linguistic and cultural problems as well as the checklist of pronunciation skills in *Well Said* (Grant, 2001) to track Kim Su's progress.
- Ms. Rogers will evaluate two areas of language: accuracy of pronunciation and social communication skills. She uses a text that has built-in tests, allowing her to rely on the book as a means of evaluating and marking progress in pronunciation.

- She will compile a portfolio of audiotapes, write observations, and have Kim Su keep self-evaluation charts to evaluate and chart progress in the use of social language.

Observe and Reflect

1. Choose the way or ways of evaluating your student that are most helpful to you. You may even devise your own informal method after you understand what evaluation means. If the method you choose is burdensome or not helpful, do not be afraid to change it.

2. Keep notes on your student. These notes will benefit you by helping you remember from one session to the next what the student has covered and knows.

Skill Checklist

Student: Check (✔) and date as behavior is observed.			
Observed skills	Date	Date	Date

Portfolio for Tutoring Sessions

Student:
Dates covered:

Entry	Date	Date	Date

Self-Evaluation Chart

Name:	
What I want to learn	What I have learned

CHAPTER  11

"What can I do if the student shows little progress?"

**Identify the student's problems;
seek help for specific needs.**

You have evaluated your students' progress; you know how much they have learned, and you see their strengths and weaknesses. However, you are disappointed that they have not made the progress you expected, and they are still making mistakes on topics you have covered thoroughly in tutoring sessions.

It is perfectly normal for students to have significantly less than 100% recall. Consider it a sign of progress if they recognize their own mistakes in grammar or pronunciation before you point them out. We have covered cultural, linguistic, and personal factors that can inhibit progress in chapter 6; now that you have encountered these problems in your tutoring situation, you need solutions. If you are sure you have carefully followed all the guidelines in this text (summarized in the Skill Checklist for students in chapter 10 and the Tutor Performance Checklist in chapter 12), reteach the skill(s) your students have not mastered.

Reteaching means teaching a skill you have already taught by presenting it in a different way. Here are some ways you can create variety:

- Change and simplify the words you originally used to present the skill.
- In a book, in a magazine, or on the Internet, find charts, pictures, and other visual aids you did not use the first time.

- Find activities that use more than one of the five senses. In other words, find written, oral, and hands-on activities that reinforce the skill you are reteaching.

Here are some additional troubleshooting approaches to use if your students' problems persist. Remember that patience and practice are the key to progress in a second language.

Reteach to Linguistic Factors

Suppose you are working with an adult Japanese male who is having trouble mastering certain sounds in English pronunciation.

1. Make a list of some of the specific problems you have been working on with your student without success. For example, your Japanese student may have difficulty hearing the difference between /l/ as in *lake* and /r/ as in *rake*.

2. Look for a text on the Internet, in the library, or in a university bookstore that discusses potential pronunciation difficulties for Japanese speakers. One example is *Learner English* (Swan & Smith, 2001), which describes grammar and pronunciation problems common to several ethnic groups that ESL teachers and tutors frequently encounter.

3. Find a pronunciation exercise in a textbook or Internet source that gives techniques for helping with the problem.

4. If possible, contact an ESL professional in a local school or on the Internet for advice.

Do not become discouraged if progress is still not immediate. It often takes many hours of practice both inside and outside your tutoring classroom for a student to master a sound in English that does not exist in the student's native language. Do not introduce new material until your student shows some competency with old material.

In summary, you can solve linguistic problems in speaking, grammar, and writing by following these general guidelines:

1. Identify the specific problem.
2. Research problems common to your students' ethnic group.
3. Find sources that deal with the problem.
4. Consult with an ESL expert if necessary.

Remember that the goal in teaching English pronunciation is to make the students' speech comprehensible to other English speakers, not to erase their native accent. Also keep in mind that a speech impediment, such as a lisp, may be the cause of a student's problem.

Reteach to Cultural Factors

Sometimes lack of progress is not linked to finding the right teaching method but to understanding the student's native culture. Suppose that you are working with a girl from India who always wears the traditional Indian sari to class. In addition, she always says "Yes" when you ask her if she understands you, but her homework is usually incomplete or poorly done. She also appears to be reluctant to do the activities you prepare for her in class.

- Consider the student's cultural background, and look for a source that describes the lifestyle of women in India. Her responsibilities in a traditional Indian home may be the reason her homework is often incomplete.

- Research the education system of her native country to see what kinds of activities students, especially females, typically do there. You might check *Culturegrams* (2001), do an Internet search, consult an embassy, or look at a guide to international customs (often found in the business section of bookstores). Perhaps you have inadvertently asked her to do something that is taboo in her culture.

- Ask her why she cannot do her homework and what kind of activities she likes to do.

- Adjust your class to accommodate whatever problem you see. For example, allow time for her to finish her homework under your supervision before she leaves your class. Find activities she can do to show she understands you.

- Use activities and materials that reflect what she does at home. For example, if she does a lot of cooking, ask her to explain a recipe in both written and oral form. Ask her to bring the ingredients to class and show how she would prepare the recipe. These activities would allow you to check grammar, writing, and speaking skills.

- Consider an activity that takes you out of the classroom. Perhaps it would help your student to visit a grocery store in her area.

Reteach to Personality Factors

Sometimes, although not as commonly, progress is blocked because of the students' personality and not because of a cultural or linguistic factor. Perhaps your student is a very shy female who is willing to read a story aloud but appears afraid to ask or answer any questions about the story. You may have another student from the same native culture who is very outgoing, so you do not believe it is a cultural problem. You are afraid to provide more challenging activities until the shy student demonstrates comprehension of materials used in class.

- Assure the student that you will never treat her mistakes as stupid and that you welcome questions.

- Help her enjoy the language acquisition process by giving her nonspeaking tasks that will show her comprehension without the risk of making a mistake. For example, play Simon Says, or give her commands such as

  1. Pick up the green pencil.
  2. Write your name in the upper left-hand corner of the paper.

3. Turn to the story on page 45 of your reading book.

4. Read the first paragraph silently.

5. What is the name of the girl in the story? Write it on the first line under your name on the paper.

- Introduce activities that allow her to answer questions with a simple *yes* or *no*. For example, ask, "Is the girl in the story sad? Does she have many friends?"

- Model a short answer to the same questions and ask her to repeat after you: "Yes, she is." "No, she doesn't."

- Praise her when she answers correctly. Keep a smile on your face when she gives the wrong answer; in a calm voice, model the correct answer.

> Do not assume that all speakers of a particular language will have the same problems even though they are common to that ethnic group. Be aware and prepared, but do not prejudge.

Case Studies: Points of Interest

✦ Case Study 1

- Ms. Freeman uses materials and activities that are directly related to the lifestyle of the Somali women to keep them motivated.

- She reviews numbers 1–10 before introducing new material.

✦ Case Study 2

- Ms. Hawkins notes that Omar prefers hands-on activities so that she will know how to motivate him to learn if she has to reteach any material.

- She notes that he is reluctant to express his opinion, so she thinks about ways to encourage him to do this in the future.

✦ Case Study 3

- Ms. Rogers refers to *Learner English* (Swan & Smith, 2001) to locate predictable problems of native Chinese speakers.

- She discovers that the initial /l/ and /r/ sounds are a common problem for Chinese speakers who are learning English, so she prepares numerous activities to practice and reteach these sounds if necessary.

CHAPTER 12

"How can I evaluate my performance as an ESL tutor?"

Use simple self-assessment procedures.

From time to time, it is important to evaluate your own performance as well as your student's. You may wonder why your student is not progressing at the rate you would like and want to determine if you need to do something different. Or you may feel that you are doing an adequate job but want to have a method of confirming your assessment. Three ways to evaluate yourself are by getting student feedback, using a student skills checklist, and using a tutor performance checklist.

Student Feedback

Students may give feedback by means of a direct comment. For example, a student may say that something you did in one of your sessions really helped with success outside your class. Always write down such comments to help you with future self-evaluations and with accountability to those who are paying for your services or expect you to deliver results. If the student seems reluctant or unable to perform a task you have assigned, ask if the student would prefer another activity. Make these notes on the Student Information Card (see chapter 1) or in your lesson planning book.

Student Skills Checklist

Feedback may also come from measurable improvement in the skills you have worked on. For example, if you are trying to help your student improve grades in a social studies class, improved quiz and test scores will indicate your success. Keep a record of all quiz and test scores as you work with the student. If possible, make a copy of each test so you can become familiar with the student's mistakes and help the student correct them. If you are working on a language skill, create a checklist for the student and check off each skill as it is mastered.

Tutor Performance Checklist

As an untrained or inexperienced tutor of ESL, you may have difficulty deciding which parts of this text apply to you and your tutoring situation. Assume that you need all of them, and review each one carefully. The section that you might be inclined to overlook may be the very one you need most to be successful with your student.

Based on the previous 11 chapters, create a checklist to be sure you are covering all the basics that help you in working with an ESL student, or use the checklist provided as a reproducible form at the end of this chapter.

Complete the checklist. If you feel you are deficient in any of the areas listed, go back to the sections of *PACE Yourself* that discusses those topics. Before tutoring a student, try the unit activities below to review and practice the skills described in each unit.

Unit Activities

◆ Unit 1: Prepare
- List the advantages and disadvantages of working with the age group you are most likely to work with.
- Make a shopping list (see chapter 2) of things you will need in order to teach the age group you have selected.

◆ Unit 2: Assess
- Choose the case study that represents the age group you selected in the Unit 1 activity. List the personal, emotional, and cultural factors of the student(s) in the case study.
- From the information given in the case study, list the student's needs and determine his or her level (i.e., beginning, intermediate, advanced).

◆ Unit 3: Construct
- Choose the case study that most closely resembles your own tutoring situation. Plan the next 1-hour lesson for the student(s) in the case study you selected (see the Lesson Planning Sheet in chapter 7).

✦ Unit 4: Evaluate

- Generate a checklist for the student in the case study you selected.
- Choose the type of progress documentation that you think would work best in this tutoring situation.

Case Studies: Points of Interest

✦ Case Study 1

- Mrs. Freeman documents learning behaviors such as *reluctant to speak* and *participates willingly* and will later determine if these behaviors are personal or cultural.

✦ Case Study 2

- Ms. Hawkins uses her list of Omar's weaknesses as a checklist for the pronunciation and reading skills to work on in future lessons.
- She uses Omar's classroom behavior to evaluate the success of her lesson (e.g., "Omar was attentive throughout the lesson. He was not afraid to ask questions.").

✦ Case Study 3

- Ms. Rogers will use feedback from Kim Su about her meetings with other women in the church to determine progress in social skills.
- Ms. Rogers regards her ability to establish a rapport with Kim Su as a sign that her class has been successful.

> As the case studies show, evaluation is a process that begins on the first day of class and continues until the last session. This continuous process guarantees that you will remain aware of your student's changing needs and abilities. Experience will soon enable you to evaluate and adapt quickly to your students' needs and take pride in their accomplishments.

Observe and Reflect

Create a checklist you could use to determine reading skills. Refer to the reading lesson plan in chapter 7 and the General Guidelines for Literacy Skill Levels in chapter 4.

Tutor Performance Checklist

Prepare	✓
Am I familiar with activities appropriate for the student's age?	
Do I sufficiently understand the student's own background, problems, and goals?	
Do I have appropriate materials for the student to work with?	
Do I know how to organize lessons so the student can follow them easily?	
Assess	
Do I know the student's language level so I can plan lessons that are not too easy or too difficult?	
Do I know how to use my assessment of the student's needs and goals to select the best types of activities? (See chapter 5, Table 2.)	
Do I understand personal, cultural, and linguistic elements that may affect the student's behavior or willingness to perform the tasks I choose? (See chapter 1.)	
Construct	
Am I using all the information I obtained about my student in the Prepare and Assess stages to create meaningful lesson plans?	
Have I chosen the best lesson plan format to meet my student's goals?	
Are my lesson plans appropriate for my student's language level?	
Am I using visual aids, such as graphs, charts, and pictures, to make lessons interesting and comprehensible?	
Evaluate	
Am I keeping a good record of my student's progress?	
Am I using all available resources that can help my student?	
Am I giving my student enough opportunity to express ideas and concerns?	

References

Baker, A., & Goldstein, S. (1990). *Pronunciation pairs: An introductory course for students of English*. New York: Cambridge University Press.

Baldrige, L. (1993). *Letitia Baldrige's new complete guide to executive manners*. New York: Rawson Associates.

Carver, T. K., & Fotinos, S. D. (1997). *A conversation book: English in everyday life* (3rd ed.). Englewood Cliffs, NJ: Prentice Hall.

Crossroads café [Videotape series]. (2001). Alexandria, VA: PBS Adult Learning Service. Available from http://www.pbs.org/als/crossroads.

Culturegrams. (2001). Brigham Young University. Provo, UT: David M. Kennedy Center for International Studies Publication Services. Available from http://www.culturegrams.com.

ESL Flashcards. (n.d.). Boggle's World. Retrieved June 17, 2002, from http://bogglesworld.com/cards.htm.

Graham, C. (1978). *Jazz chants*. New York: Oxford University Press.

Graham, C. (1986). *Small talk*. New York: Oxford University Press.

Graham, C. (2001). *Jazz chants old and new*. New York: Oxford University Press.

Graham, C. R., & Walsh, M. M. (1996). *Adult education ESL teachers guide*. Kingsville: Texas A&I University. Retrieved May 31, 2002, from http://humanities.byu.edu/elc/Teacher/TeacherGuideMain.

Grant, L. (2001). *Well said: Pronunciation for clear communication* (2nd ed.). Boston: Heinle & Heinle.

Johnston, I. (2000). *Essays and arguments, section two*. Retrieved June 6, 2002, from http://www.mala.bc.ca/~johnstoi/arguments/argument2.htm.

Kirn, E., & Hartmann, P. (1990). *Interactions II: A reading skills book*. New York: McGraw-Hill.

de Maupassant, G. (1996). The necklace. In B. Goodman, *English, YES! Learning English through literature: Intermediate level 2* (pp. 71–87). Lincolnwood, IL: Jamestown. (Original work published 1907)

The New Oxford Picture Dictionary CD-ROM [Computer software]. (1997). Oxford: Oxford University Press.

Pearson Adult Learning Centre. (2002a). *Assignment archive: Basic composition*. Retrieved February 8, 2002, from http://palc.sd40.bc.ca/palc/Archive/assignme.htm.

Pearson Adult Learning Centre. (2002b). *English resources*. New Westminster, British Columbia, Canada: New Westminster School District. Retrieved May 31, 2002, from http://palc.sd40.bc.ca/palc/resource.htm.

Pearson Adult Learning Centre. (2002c). *Tips for writers*. New Westminster, British Columbia, Canada: New Westminster School District. Retrieved May 31, 2002, from http://palc.sd40.bc.ca/palc/tipsfor.htm.

Probst, G. W. (1999). *Best teacher description*. Retrieved August 14, 2002, from http://humanities.byu.edu/elc/teacher/bestteacher.

The Rosetta Stone [Computer software]. (2000). Harrison, VA: Fairfield Language Technologies.

Shapiro, N., & Adelson-Goldstein, J. (1998). *The Oxford picture dictionary*. New York: Oxford University Press.

State education agencies. (2002). Washington, DC: U.S. Department of Education. Retrieved June 6, 2002, from http://www.ed.gov/Programs/bastmp/SEA.htm.

Stavrianos, L. S., Andrews, L. K., McLane, J. R., Safford, F. R., & Sheridan, J. E. (1979). *A global history*. Boston: Allyn & Bacon.

Stern, K. (Ed.). (1997). *Longman dictionary of American English*. White Plains, NY: Addison Wesley Longman.

Swan, M., & Smith, B. (2001). *Learner English: A teacher's guide to interference and other problems*. New York: Cambridge University Press.

APPENDIX A:
Texts, Web Sites, and Other Resources for ESL Tutors

Cultural References

Baldrige, L. (1993). *Letitia Baldrige's new complete guide to executive manners*. New York: Rawson Associates.

Culturegrams. (2001). Provo, UT: Brigham Young University, David M. Kennedy Center for International Studies Publication Services. Available from http://www.culturegrams.com.
   Culturegrams are available for most countries around the world. Each describes the history, customs, and culture of a particular country.

Swan, M., & Smith, B. (2001). *Learner English: A teacher's guide to interference and other problems.* New York: Cambridge University Press.
   This practical reference guide to features of various languages can help you understand some of your students' language problems.

ESL Dictionaries

✦ Beginning–Intermediate Level

The New Oxford Picture Dictionary CD-ROM [Computer software]. (1997). Oxford: Oxford University Press.

For ages 10–adult, beginning–intermediate level, this program complements The Oxford Picture Dictionary *(Shapiro & Adelson-Goldstein, 1998) with thematic contact that includes job skills information.*

Rosenthal, M. S., Freeman, D. B., Fuchs, M., & Rosenthal, J. N. (1987). *Longman photo dictionary.* White Plains, NY: Longman.

Designed for beginners, this vocabulary and conversation book presents view of language and life in North America through photographs. Classroom activities range from listening, writing, and grammar practice to storytelling and discussions.

Shapiro, N., & Adelson-Goldstein, J. (1998). *The Oxford picture dictionary.* New York: Oxford University Press.

This dictionary is good for teaching beginning- to intermediate-level students commonly used nouns, verbs, adjectives, and prepositions. Supplemental workbooks and a teacher's manual facilitate preparation of lessons for students with minimal English skills.

✦ Intermediate–Advanced Level

Cambridge dictionary of American English. (2000). New York: Cambridge University Press.

This English-English dictionary is designed especially for students of ESL at the intermediate level and above. Definitions are written in easy-to-understand English, and entries often include sentences using the word to help students with correct usage. An accompanying CD is available.

Hornby, A. S. (Ed.). (2000). *Oxford advanced learner's dictionary* (6th ed.). New York: Oxford University Press.

This widely used dictionary, good for advanced learners in academic programs, includes more than 80,000 references for both British and American English.

Stern, K. (Ed.). (1997). *Longman dictionary of American English.* White Plains, NY: Addison Wesley Longman.

This English-English dictionary for students at or above the intermediate level contains 44,000 entries with illustrations, grammatical information, and spelling rules. Sample sentences clarify meaning and usage.

✦ All Levels

Grammars and language courses. (2001). Retrieved May 31, 2002, from http://www.yourdictionary.com/grammars.html.

Links to grammars of many of the world's languages are featured on this site.

iLoveLanguages. http://www.ilovelanguages.com.
> *This site houses a universal translator.*

Kantola, H. (2002). *Dictionaries on the Web.* Helsinki, Finland: Author. Retrieved May 31, 2002, from http://www.helsinki.fi/~hkantola/dict.html.
> *This page lists various links to dictionaries on the Web.*

Language Discovery [Computer software]. (n.d.) Atlanta, GA: World of Reading.
> *For ages 8–18, this program helps students learn 1,000 words covering more than 30 topics. It includes an online dictionary and two games.*

The Newbury House Online Dictionary. http://nhd.heinle.com.
> *This online dictionary is a helpful resource for tutors and students.*

ESL Grammar Books

✦ Beginning Level

Azar, B. S. (1996). *Basic English grammar* (2nd ed.). Upper Saddle River, NJ: Prentice Hall Regents.
> *This popular grammar text is the first in a series by Azar.*

Butler, L., & Pednecky, J. (2000). *Grammar links 1: A theme-based course for reference and practice.* Boston: Houghton Mifflin.
> *Designed for low beginning–level ESL courses, this is the first volume in a theme-based series using a communicative approach but focusing on structure.*

Elbaum, S. N. (2001). *Grammar in context 1* (3rd ed.). Boston: Heinle & Heinle.
> *The text, the first in a three-text series, provides comprehensive explanations, culturally rich readings, and a variety of writing activities.*

Foley, B. H., & Neblett, E. R. (1998). *The new grammar in action 1: An integrated course in English.* Boston: Heinle & Heinle.
> *This book is the high beginning–level text in the New Grammar in Action series, which uses a communicative approach to language learning. The series integrates listening, speaking, writing, and reading practice.*

Foley, B., & Neblett, E. R. (2001). *Basic grammar in action: An integrated course in English.* Boston: Heinle & Heinle.
> *This true beginning-level program provides a good foundation for students, progressing from vocabulary development to sentence-level grammatical instruction.*

✦ Intermediate Level

Azar, B. S. (1992). *Fundamentals of English grammar* (2nd ed.). Englewood Cliffs, NJ: Prentice Hall Regents.
> *This grammar text features charts and both oral and written exercises in a developmental approach.*

Elbaum, S. N. (2001). *Grammar in context 2* (3rd ed.). Boston: Heinle & Heinle.

> *This text, the second in a three-text series, provides comprehensive explanations, culturally rich readings, and a variety of writing activities.*

Foley, B. H., & Neblett, E. R. (1998). *The new grammar in action 2: An integrated course in English*. Boston: Heinle & Heinle.

> *This is the second text in the New Grammar in Action series, which uses a communicative approach to language learning. The series integrates listening, speaking, writing, and reading practice.*

Mahnke, M. K., & O'Dowd, E. (1999). *Grammar links 2: A theme-based course for reference and practice*. Boston: Houghton Mifflin.

> *This is the second volume in a theme-based series using a communicative approach but focusing on structure.*

Raimes, A. (1992). *Grammar troublespots: An editing guide for students* (2nd ed.). New York: St. Martin's Press.

> *This book is designed to help advanced students with problems that occur frequently in writing.*

✦ Advanced Level

Azar, B. S. (1999). *Understanding and using English grammar* (3rd ed.). Upper Saddle River, NJ: Prentice Hall Regents.

> *Appropriate for intermediate- and advanced-level students, this grammar text contains the useful charts found in Azar's other grammar texts.*

Elbaum, S. N. (2001). *Grammar in context 3* (3rd ed.). Boston: Heinle & Heinle.

> *This text, the third in a three-text series, provides comprehensive explanations, culturally rich readings, and a variety of writing activities.*

Foley, B. H., & Neblett, E. R. (1998). *The new grammar in action 3: An integrated course in English*. Boston: Heinle & Heinle.

> *This is the high intermediate– to low advanced–level text in the New Grammar in Action series, which uses a communicative approach to language learning. The series integrates listening, speaking, writing, and reading practice.*

Steer, J., & Carlisi, K. (1997). *The advanced grammar book* (2nd ed.). Boston: Heinle & Heinle.

> *Designed for both preuniversity and nonacademic learners of English, this text provides the student with a analysis of English grammar.*

Van Zante, J. (2000). *Grammar links 3: A theme-based course for reference and practice*. Boston: Houghton Mifflin.

> *This is the third volume in a theme-based series using a communicative approach but focusing on structure.*

Ziemer, M. (1999). *Grammar contexts: A resource guide for interactive practice*. Ann Arbor: University of Michigan Press.

> *This resource book offers activities and lesson plans that connect grammatical structures to situations and topics.*

Azar, B. S. (1995). *Chartbook: A reference grammar*. Englewood Cliffs, NJ: Prentice Hall Regents.

> *This text summarizes many important grammar structures in user-friendly charts.*

Rinvolucri, M. (1984). *Grammar games: Cognitive, affective, and drama activities for EFL students*. New York: Cambridge University Press.

> *This book is an excellent resource for games that teach and practice structure.*

Rinvolucri, M., & Davis, P. (1995). *More grammar games: Cognitive, affective, and movement activities for EFL students*. New York: Cambridge University Press.

> *This is another source for activities that teach grammar through games.*

English Idiom Texts and References

✦ Beginning–Intermediate Level

The American heritage dictionary of idioms for students of English. (2000). Boston: Houghton Mifflin.

> *Students might use this up-to-date dictionary as a reference while they read various texts.*

Dixson, R. (1994). *Essential idioms in English*. Englewood Cliffs, NJ: Regents/Prentice Hall.

> *This classic text highlights and practices the use of common idioms in English.*

Feare, R. (1996). *Everyday idioms for reference and practice*. White Plains, NY: Longman.

> *This book covers some of the idioms most commonly used in everyday speech.*

Huizenga, J. (1999). *Can you believe it? Stories and idioms from real life* (Books 1–3). New York: Oxford University Press.

> *This three-level series, which integrates reading, listening, and speaking skills, covers idioms, two-word verbs, and common expressions through tales from around the globe.*

ESL Listening/Speaking Texts

✦ Beginning–Intermediate Level

Baker, A., & Goldstein, S. (1990). *Pronunciation pairs: An introductory course for students of English*. New York: Cambridge University Press.

> *Each unit of this text has students practice a different sound in English through a variety of activities.*

Boyd, J. R., & Boyd, M. A. (1991). *Before book one: Listening activities for pre-beginning-level students of English* (2nd ed.). Englewood Cliffs, NJ: Prentice Hall Regents.

> *This book answers a need for tutors of students who are absolute beginners and need practice in listening and responding to English. It teaches beginning-level students to recognize and produce the sounds of American English.*

Carver, T. K., & Fotinos, S. D. (1997). *A conversation book: English in everyday life* (3rd ed.). Englewood Cliffs, NJ: Prentice Hall.

> *The book helps students develop conversational fluency and some basic writing skills.*

Gilbert, J. B. (2001). *Clear speech from the start: Basic pronunciation and listening comprehension in North American English* (Student's book). New York: Cambridge University Press.

> *This text, which stresses rhythm, intonation, and sound as grammar cues, is designed to give beginning-level students help in pronunciation.*

Heyer, S. (1989). *Picture stories for beginning-level communication* (2nd ed.). Englewood Cliffs, NJ: Prentice Hall.

> *For students of all ages, the text uses picture stories to teach vocabulary, grammar, and writing.*

Richards, J. C. (n.d.). *Springboard.* Oxford: Oxford University Press. Retrieved May 31, 2002, from http://www1.oup.co.uk/elt/springboard.

> *Springboard is an online textbook for communication.*

✦ Intermediate–Advanced Level

Gilbert, J. B. (1993). *Clear speech: Pronunciation and listening comprehension in North American English* (Student's book, 2nd ed.). New York: Cambridge University Press.

> *This well-known pronunciation book focuses on areas that contribute most to intelligibility.*

Grant, L. (2001). *Well said: Pronunciation for clear communication* (2nd ed.). Boston: Heinle & Heinle.

> *This very helpful pronunciation text works well within a tutoring environment. Students assess their own errors and work on areas that are most problematic.*

Leshinsky, J. G. (1995). *Authentic listening and discussion for advanced students.* Englewood Cliffs, NJ: Prentice Hall Regents.

> *As the title suggests, with this book students can practice oral/aural skills through the use of authentic texts.*

✦ All Levels

Graham, C. (1978). *Jazz chants.* New York: Oxford University Press.

> *This book introduced the use of chants and jazz rhythms to help students practice spoken sounds and intonations of English.*

Graham, C. (1986). *Small talk.* New York: Oxford University Press.

> *This collection has students practice various language functions through chants.*

Graham, C. (2001). *Jazz chants old and new.* New York: Oxford University Press.

> *This edition contains the best of Graham's jazz chants along with some new ones.*

Readers

✦ Beginning Level

Heyer, S. True stories [series]. New York: Longman.
Designed for adult readers, the books in this series contain high-interest material.

Zaffran, B., & Krulik, D. (1993). *Starting English with a smile.* New York: McGraw-Hill Contemporary.
This reader is part of a three-book series that uses short stories to help students develop vocabulary and comprehension.

✦ Beginning–Intermediate Level

Broukal, M., & Murphy, P. The USA series. New York: Longman.
These readers examines the people, places, and customs of the United States.

Cambridge English readers [series]. Cambridge: Cambridge University Press.
This large collection includes readers at various word-count levels with topics suitable and of high interest to adults and young adults.

✦ High Beginning–Low Advanced Level

Blanchard, K. L., & Root, C. B. (1995–2000). *For your information* (Books 1–4). White Plains, NY: Longman.

✦ High Intermediate–Advanced Level

Baudoin, E. M., Dobson, B. K., Bober, E. S., Clarke, M. A., & Silberstein, S. (1994). *Reader's choice* (3rd ed.). Ann Arbor: University of Michigan Press.
This text offers readings on many topics and in many genres to build vocabulary and reading comprehension skills for different purposes.

Earle-Carlin, S., & Hildebrand, C. (Eds.). (2000). *American perspectives.* White Plains, NY: Longman.
This theme-based reader presents views of U.S. culture through material selected from books, newspapers, magazines, and Web sites.

✦ All Levels

Goodman, B. English, YES! [series]. Lincolnwood, IL: Jamestown.
This series offers an anthology of readings (many adapted from or in the original form of well-known authors) for readers of each level and incorporates grammar, vocabulary, and communication activities to develop reading comprehension.

✦ Content Area Texts

Christison, M. (1993). *Social studies: Content and learning strategies.* Reading, MA: Addison-Wesley.

> This text integrates content-area reading comprehension, vocabulary, and activities to help middle school and high school students with limited English skills succeed in mainstream social studies classes.

Iwamoto, J. (1994). *Coming together: Integrating math and language.* Upper Saddle River, NJ: Prentice Hall Regents.

> This two-part text teaches math concepts and vocabulary and helps students understand the language of story problems.

Johnston, J., & Johnston, M. (1990). *Content points: Science, mathematics, and social studies* (Books A, B, and C). Reading, MA: Addison-Wesley.

> This series uses activities based on the cognitive academic language learning approach (CALLA) to teach the language students need to succeed in school.

ESL Integrated Series

✦ Beginning–Intermediate Level

Crossroads [series]. New York: Oxford University Press.
> This series, designed for adult and high school students, uses a competency-based approach with grammatical objectives.

Graham, C. R., & Walsh, M. M. (1996). *Adult education ESL teachers guide.* Kingsville: Texas A&I University. Retrieved May 31, 2002, from http://humanities.byu.edu/elc/Teacher/TeacherGuideMain.
> This complete text includes lesson plans, exercise sheets, and teaching techniques for beginning-level, intermediate-level, and illiterate adults.

Molinsky, S., & Bliss, B. (2000). *Side by side* (3rd ed.). Englewood Cliffs, NJ: Prentice Hall.
> This series uses guided conversation to teach grammar and communication skills.

Whitney, N., & McKeegan, D. (1998). *Open house.* New York: Oxford University Press.
> This text appeals to preteens and young teens through its design and subject matter. It uses a communicative skills approach.

✦ Beginning–Advanced Level

Crossroads café [Videotape]. (2001). Alexandria, VA: PBS Adult Learning Service. Available from http://www.pbs.org/als/crossroads.
> *Crossroads Café* is a complete language program that teaches English by depicting the lives of six characters and their challenges and struggles, which are typical of many ESL learners.

Interactions/mosaic [series] (4th ed., 2001). New York: McGraw-Hill Contemporary.
This five-level, four-skill series, designed for academic students, includes many interactive and communicative activities.

Macero, J. D., & Lane, M. A. (1977). *Laubach way to English*. Syracuse, NY: New Readers Press.
This book is the ESL teaching version of the famous Laubach way to literacy.

Richards, J. C. New interchange: English for international communication [series]. New York: Cambridge University Press.
Considered one of the most popular series worldwide, the books cover the beginning to the intermediate level and integrate skills using real-world topics. The series offers a number of support materials.

Richards, J., & Sandy, C. Passages: An upper-level multiskills course [series]. New York: Cambridge University Press.
This two-level multiskills series follows New Interchange and brings students from the high intermediate to the advanced level. It uses a communicative approach and focuses on fluency and accuracy.

The Rosetta Stone [Computer software]. (2000). Harrison, VA: Fairfield Language Technologies. Available from http://www.rosettastone.com.
Language learning software on CD-ROM and online, the Rosetta Stone is designed to help students develop language skills at their own pace. See also the companion Web site.

Rost, M. Longman English online: An interactive course for global communication [series]. White Plains, NY: Pearson Education.
This beginning- to advanced-level video-based series uses a combination of CD-ROM and online instruction.

Writing Texts

◆ Beginning Level

Chabot, A. M. (2000). *Starts with A: A beginner's guide to the alphabet*. Lewiston, NY: Full Blast Productions.
This activity book introduces the letters of the alphabet and is suitable for all ages.

Haynes, J. (n.d.). *American handwriting: Slow and easy*. McHenry, IL: Delta Systems.
American Handwriting was developed for learners in the workplace or classroom who do not read or write the Roman alphabet.

Reid, J. (1996). *Basic writing* (2nd ed.). Upper Saddle River, NJ: Prentice Hall Regents.
This book is designed for students whose writing skills lag behind their other skills, such as listening and speaking.

✦ Beginning–Intermediate Level

Blanchard, K. L., & Root, C. B. Ready to write [series]. New York: Longman.
This series of three writing texts (Get Ready to Write, Ready to Write, and Ready to Write More) takes the students from basic sentence writing to paragraphs and essay writing with a wealth of writing activities.

Miller, J., & Cohen, R. (2001). *Reason to write: Strategies for success in academic writing.* New York: Oxford University Press.
The text, designed for low intermediate–level students, uses a process approach in theme-based units and includes readings and many writing tasks.

✦ Intermediate Level

Boardman, C., & Frydenberg, G. (2001). *Writing to communicate.* New York: Longman.
The text centers around three themes—milestones, ecology, and relationships—and guides students from paragraph to essay writing.

✦ Advanced Level

Macdonald, A., & Macdonald, G. (1996). *Mastering writing essentials.* White Plains, NY: Pearson ESL.
Designed for the intermediate through the advanced level, the text covers the types of writing skills expected of learners at these levels.

Reid, J. (2000). *The process of composition* (3rd ed.). White Plains, NY: Prentice Hall Regents.
This text focuses on academic writing and includes information on using library as well as online sources.

Scull, S. (1987). *Critical reading and writing for advanced ESL students.* Englewood Cliffs, NJ: Prentice Hall.
This text exposes students to various rhetorical modes and features various genres.

English for Specific Purposes Texts

Bartell, K. H. (1995). *American business English.* Ann Arbor: University of Michigan Press.
The text highlights basic strategies and techniques for successful business writing.

Lee, D., Hall, C., & Hurley, M. (1991). *American legal English: Using language in legal contexts.* Ann Arbor: University of Michigan Press.
This text provides nonnative speakers of English with an introduction to the U.S. legal system.

Lites, E., & Thorpe, K. (2001). *English for global business.* Ann Arbor: University of Michigan Press.
This textbook focuses on oral English communication skills, particularly those that are most needed for international business.

Maher, J. C. (1992). *International medical communication in English*. Ann Arbor: University of Michigan Press.

> *This reference, designed for medical personnel or students who do not speak English as a first language, covers effective communication strategies in various medical situations.*

Survival Skills Texts

Foley, B., & Pomann, H. (1992). *Lifelines* (2nd ed., Books 1–4). White Plains, NY: Pearson ESL.

> *This four-volume, competency-based series combines real-life skills with language study.*

Mosteller, L., Paul, B., & Haight, M. (1994). *Survival English: English through conversations* (Books 1–3). White Plains, NY: Pearson ESL.

> *This three-level series covers the beginning to the intermediate level and is designed to help adult students develop language and coping skills for everyday living.*

Newman, C. M., Grognet, A. G., & Crandall, J. A. (1993). *LifePrints: ESL for adults*. Syracuse, NY: New Readers Press.

> *This three-level series is designed to develop the language skills of adult students in survival and job situations. It takes the student from the low beginning to the low intermediate level.*

Real-life English: A competency-based ESL program for adults. (1994). Austin, TX: Raintree Steck-Vaughn.

> *This interactive, four-level program takes the adult ESL learner from preliteracy to the intermediate level while providing practice in life-skill competencies.*

Web Sites for ESL Tutors

✦ ESL Sites

Comenius English language center. http://www.comenius.com.

> *This Web site provides access to materials, lessons, and products.*

Dave's ESL café. http://www.eslcafe.com.

> *Helpful hints, interesting items, and the joke of the day are found here along with many enjoyable aids for the ESL teacher.*

English Club ESL worksheets. http://www.englishclub.net/handouts/index.htm.

> *This site provides handouts in listening, speaking, reading, writing, grammar, vocabulary, and pronunciation.*

English page. http://www.englishpage.com.

> *This site is most appropriate for high school to adult students. It contains tutorials on topics including vocabulary, verbs, and prepositions; samples of literature; and articles on business and science topics.*

ESL Magazine. http://www.eslmag.com.
> *The site offers free information and the opportunity to subscribe to the publication.*

ESL resources, games, songs, chat and books. (2002). Retrieved May 31, 2002, from http://www.nanana.com/esl.html.
> *This page contains links to sources for each topic listed in the title as well as for lesson plans and activities.*

ForumEnglish. http://www.forumeducation.net.
> *This site offers student exercises and tests plus materials for teachers. You may log on as a visitor to see if this interests you, but eventually you will have to pay to join the "forum." It may be worthwhile if you see materials you like.*

free-ENGLISH. http://www.freeenglish.com.
> *This free, high-quality online resource targets ESL students and teachers.*

Mathé, E. (2002). *English tests and quizzes: Practice for students of English.* Retrieved May 31, 2002, from http://www.englishlearner.com/tests/test.html.
> *This site offers helpful quizzes to evaluate students and give them extra practice.*

Self-study quizzes for ESL students. (2002). Retrieved May 31, 2002, from http://iteslj.org/quizzes.
> *At this site, students can take and score quizzes on grammar points, job-hunting skills, reading comprehension, and other topics.*

Tanguay, E. (n.d.). *Language teaching.* Retrieved May 31, 2002, from http://www.tanguay.info/site.aspx?s=teach.
> *This site contains links to resources such as listening files and texts.*

✦ General Education Sites

DiscoverySchool. (2002). Silver Spring, MD: Discovery Communications. Retrieved May 31, 2002, from http://school.discovery.com/schoolhome.html.
> *This Web site, produced by the company that owns the Discovery Channel, contains lesson plans, teaching tools, a clipart gallery, and a puzzlemaker.*

ERIC Clearinghouse on Reading, English, and Communications. (2002). Bloomington, IN: U.S. Department of Education and the National Library of Education. Retrieved May 31, 2002, from http://www.indiana.edu/~eric_rec.
> *This site is dedicated to providing educational materials, services, and course work to anyone interested in the language arts. The site also provides a free question-and-answer service.*

Global schoolhouse. http://www.gsh.org.
> *The Global Schoolhouse offers a wealth of resources for teachers.*

Knowledge network explorer. http://www.kn.pacbell.com.
> *This site provides free online learning activities, tools, and resources.*

Schoolhouse. (2002). Redmond, WA: Microsoft. Retrieved May 31, 2002, from http://www.encarta.msn.com/schoolhouse/default.asp.
> *On this Web site, you can search for lessons by subject, grade level, or key word.*

✦ Online Material Sources

Freeman, G. (n.d.). *Graphic organizer index*. Retrieved May 31, 2002, from http://www.graphic.org/goindex.html.
> *See this site for examples of this helpful teaching device.*

Hewitt, I. (2002). *Free edutainment games*. Retrieved May 31, 2002, from http://www2.gol.com/users/language/games.html.
> *From this site, teachers can gain access to 100 pages of multilevel edutainment activities that are ready to photocopy.*

Home-buying guide. http://www.homebuyingguide.com.
> *This site, sponsored by the Fannie Mae Foundation, allows the downloading of information on buying homes in many languages.*

Royalty-free clip art collection for foreign/second language instruction. (2001). West Lafayette, IN: Purdue University, Department of Foreign Languages and Literatures, Center for Technology Enhanced Language Learning. Retrieved May 31, 2002, from http://www.sla.purdue.edu/fll/JapanProj/FLClipart/.
> *This Web site is a collection of simple line drawings that illustrate commonly used verbs, adjectives, and nouns.*

SparkNotes. http://www.sparknotes.com.
> *Appropriate for students in middle school and high school, this site includes study guides for literature and many other academic subjects, complete texts of classic literature, and news articles on many topics.*

World of reading. http://www.wor.com.
> *This site is a good source for ESL software.*

✦ Web Guides

Byrd, P. (2001). *English grammar on the Web*. Atlanta: Georgia State University. Retrieved May 31, 2002, from http://www.gsu.edu/~wwwesl/egw/index1.htm.
> *This site offers links to grammar exercises.*

Chareonsup, K. (2001). *The ESL center*. Ann Arbor, MI: Author. Retrieved May 31, 2002, from http://members.aol.com/eslkathy/esl.htm.
> *This page lists links to exercises in pronunciation and conversation, listening, grammar, reading and writing, and vocabulary; to sources for games, business English materials, dictionaries, music lyrics, newspapers and magazines; and to television and radio sites.*

Great sites. (2001). Chicago: American Library Association, Great Web Sites Committee. Retrieved May 31, 2002, from http://www.ala.org/parentspage/greatsites/amazing.html.
> *Sponsored by the American Library Association, this site includes links to sites on topics designed mainly for children and adolescents.*

Levine, M. (2002). *ESL plans and resources.* Northridge: California State University. Retrieved May 31, 2002, from http://www.csun.edu/~hcedu013/eslplans.html.
> *This page contains links to sources for ESL lesson plans and activities and provides a description of what each source contains.*

Levine, M. (2001). *Professional associations.* Retrieved June 10, 2002, from http://www.csun.edu/~hcedu013/eslprof.html.
> *This page provides a list of professional organizations for ESL and foreign language instructors.*

TrackStar. http://trackstar.hprtec.org.
> *Teachers can search through tracks (resource lists) set up by other teachers on all sorts of subjects by topic and grade level or set up their own tracks by filling in an online form.*

APPENDIX B:
Terminology for ESL Tutors

acculturation: process of becoming adapted to a new culture; reorientation of thinking, feeling, acting, and communicating in a new language and culture. Evidence supports the theory that social contact with the dominant culture group is very important in second language acquisition. Four stages of acculturation have been identified:

1. a period of excitement over the newness of the surroundings

2. culture shock (i.e., a feeling of intrusion of cultural differences into an individual's image of self and security)

3. a gradual recovery from culture shock; an acceptance of differences in thinking and feeling and increased empathy with others in the second culture

4. near or full recovery, either assimilation or adaptation, acceptance of the new culture, and self-confidence in the individual's new identity in the second cultur

achievement test: test directly related to particular material covered in a specified curriculum within a particular period of time.

basic interpersonal communication skills (BICS): language used in informal communication with friends to express feelings, needs, desires, and complaints in either oral or written form. Vocabulary and syntax are less complex than in formal communication. Nonnative speakers of English may appear to be good users of the language of BICS but may not do so well in the classroom. It takes approximately 2 years to achieve proficiency in BICS.

cloze test: test in which every seventh word of a passage is omitted and the student must supply a word that is correct in both content and grammar. More than one choice may be considered correct.

diagnostic test: test designed to measure proficiency in a particular aspect of a particular language. For example, a diagnostic test in writing might be devised to determine a student's problems with past tense forms.

dialogue journal: written communication between two people, usually a teacher and a student, in which the emphasis is on exchanging ideas and information. The correspondents take turns writing in the same notebook. The teacher does not comment on the students' errors but tries to stimulate the students to express themselves without feeling threatened.

discrete-point testing: testing in which language is broken down into its component parts and each part (e.g., the four skills of listening, speaking, reading, and writing) is tested individually. Other such component parts are phonology, morphology, lexicon, and syntax.

English as a foreign language (EFL): English learned by students who are living in their native country and using their native language. Their only exposure to the second language is in the classroom. They are not expected to acquire it and use it outside the classroom.

English as a second language (ESL): generic term for English learned in a country where English is spoken. ESL students need to learn English to survive in a culture that is different from that of their native country and may have little opportunity to speak their native language with people from their own culture.

English for specific purposes (ESP): English taught for particular needs (e.g., specialized vocabulary in the field of medicine, business, or travel). The goal of such classes is to facilitate use of English in a particular set of circumstances, not to enable students to achieve total mastery of English.

fossilization: point at which a language learner's competence and performance stop improving because the learner is satisfied with being able to communicate well enough or lacks the motivation to make further progress. Learners whose language level has fossilized are still in the interlanguage stage and may never advance to fluency in the second language.

General Educational Development (GED) diploma: high school equivalency diploma for those who do not complete regular high school. To qualify, students must pass a five-section test consisting of multiple-choice questions and a timed essay on an assigned topic.

Graduate Management Admission Test (GMAT©): test used by business schools to determine eligibility for admission into graduate-level business programs. The test measures abilities in the categories of verbal skills, quantitative skills, and analytical writing.

Graduate Record Examination (GRE©): standardized test required by many graduate school programs as part of entrance requirements. The General Test measures verbal, quantitative, and analytical skills. The Subject Tests are used by some graduate schools to determine qualifications for applicants in specific fields of study.

interlanguage: speaker's use of the second language before achieving fluency. Interlanguage may be comprehensible to native speakers, but it contains errors that identify the learner as a nonnative speaker.

L1: first language that a person acquire; native language; language heard since birth. From it the learner forms a concept of how language works. Barring exposure to other languages before puberty, the L1 is the language in which the learner is usually most proficient throughout life. One significant factor in the learning of the L1 is the nonthreatening, supportive environment in which it is learned.

L2: second language, in which a person may or may not acquire nativelike proficiency. Unless the L2 is learned or acquired at an early age, there is usually some interference from the L1 during the acquisition process. Many other factors influence the learner's ability to master an L2. In contrast to the former tendency to inhibit the L2 student by correcting every error, instruction now focuses on creating the kind of nonthreatening environment that the learner experienced in L1 acquisition.

language acquisition: subconscious process in which a person picks up a language; gradual emergence of language through exposure to comprehensible input that is always at a slightly higher level than the student's ability ($i + 1$). A key factor in language acquisition is lowering the *affective filter* (i.e., the emotional factors that inhibit learning) by creating a stress-free environment.

language learning: conscious process in which a learner pays attention to form and rules; deliberate effort to alter and correct one's speech in the L2. Some experts, such as Stephen Krashen, believe this approach actually inhibits the achievement of language fluency.

morphology: study of the units of meaning in a language. The smallest single unit of meaning is called a *morpheme*. A unit of meaning that can be used alone is called a *free morpheme* (e.g., *walk*). A morpheme that can never be used alone is called a *bound morpheme* (e.g., the ending *-ed*, which must be attached to a word such as *walk* to indicate an action in the past).

phonology: study of the individual units of sound in a language. The smallest unit of sound is called a *phoneme*. Each consonant and vowel is a phoneme. Some of the phonemes that exist in English do not exist in other languages, and vice versa. This sometimes causes difficulty in second language learning, and often learners will use the phoneme in the native language that is closest to but not exactly the same as a phoneme in English. For example, French lacks the *th* sound of *that* and *think*. As a result, a French speaker learning English might say *zat* or *dat* for *that* and *sink* or *tink* for *think*.

portfolio: method of evaluating student progress in which selected work produced by the student is kept in a folder as a record of what has been learned and accomplished.

proficiency test: test of global competence in a language. It is not limited to one single skill or course but covers a student's total knowledge of a language. Such tests usually consist of multiple-choice questions on grammar, vocabulary, reading and aural comprehension, and writing. The Test of English as a Foreign Language (TOEFL©) is a standardized English proficiency test.

silent period: early stage of language acquisition in which the learner may be able to indicate comprehension of language input by means of body language or gestures but is unable or reluctant to express language orally. For example, the learner may be able to respond correctly to the command "Sit!" but be reluctant to say the word *sit*. In second language acquisition, the silent period may last a year or more for children and less than a year for adults. For this reason, many language teachers like to use the total physical response (TPR) approach with beginning-level English students. See *total physical response*.

speech register: use of language in different communicative contexts. The register is affected by the audience, occasion, shared experience, and purpose of communication. For example, a successful male executive may use an entirely different vocabulary and speaking style when sitting at a conference in the board room than when watching a football game with friends.

syntax: word order in meaningful discourse. English relies heavily on syntax to convey the notions of the doer and receiver of an action. For example, there is a vast difference between *The mouse ate the cheese* and *The cheese ate the mouse.* The second sentence makes no sense because it conveys the idea that the cheese acted as an agent in the eating of a mouse.

Test of English as a Foreign Language (TOEFL©): English proficiency test that many colleges and universities require international students to take prior to admission. It consists of multiple-choice questions in grammar, reading, and listening plus a written essay.

Test of English for International Communication (TOEIC©): English proficiency test used by organizations to document employees' English proficiency and by individuals who want to demonstrate their ability to use English in the global workplace. It is a 2-hour test with multiple-choice questions (100 in listening comprehension and 100 in reading comprehension and grammar).

Test of Spoken English (TSE©): test required by some undergraduate and graduate institutions for international students. It measures the ability of nonnative speakers to communicate orally in English. The examinee listens to an audio recording and records 12 speaking activities, which may include narrating, giving directions, recommending, persuading, giving an opinion, describing, and predicting.

total physical response (TPR): teaching method that allows students to delay speech production until they feel ready. The students listen and respond physically to the teacher's commands but do not respond orally. The teacher models a command for the students, performs the action with them, and then asks them to perform the command alone. Students then learn to read and write the command. When the students are ready, they give the command for the teacher to follow. The goal of TPR is to enable the student to enjoy the experience of learning to communicate in another language, to reduce stress in the learning process, and to enable the students to acquire language the way a child does.

APPENDIX C:
Publishers in the Field of ESL

Addison Wesley Longman
1 Jacob Way
Reading, MA 01867-9984
Telephone: 800-552-2259 (K–12),
    800-322-1377 (college/adult)
Fax: 800-333-3328
http://awl.com

Alta Book Center
14 Adrian Court
Burlingame, CA 94010
Telephone: 800-ALTA-ESL
Fax: 800-ALTA-FAX
http://www.altaesl.com

Asia for Kids
Master Communications
4480 Lake Forest Drive, Suite 302
Cincinnati, OH 45242
Telephone: 800-888-9681
Fax: 513-563-3105
http://www.asiaforkids.com

Audio-Forum
96 Broad Street
Guilford, CT 06437-2612
Telephone: 800-243-1234
Fax: 888-453-4329
http://www.audioforum.com

Ballard & Tighe
PO Box 219
Brea, CA 92822-0219
Telephone: 800-321-4332
E-mail: infor@ballard-tighe.com
http://www.ballard-tighe.com

Cambridge University Press
40 West 20th Street
New York, NY 10011-4211
Telephone: 800-872-7423
Tel. 212-924-3900
Fax: 212-645-5960
http://www.cup.org

Delta Systems
1400 Miller Parkway
McHenry, IL 60050-7030
Telephone: 800-323-8270
Fax: 800-909-9901
http://www.delta-systems.com

Dominie Press
1949 Kellogg Avenue
Carlsbad, CA 92008
Telephone: 800-232-4570
Fax: 760-431-8000
http://www.dominie.com

ESL Magazine
Bridge Press
220 McKendree Avenue
Annapolis, MD 21401 USA
Telephone: 410-570-0746
Fax: 410-990-9052
http://www.eslmag.com

Harcourt College Publishers
301 Commerce Street, Suite 3700
Fort Worth, TX 76102
Tel. 817-334-7500
http://www.hbcollege.com

Heinemann
361 Hanover Street
Portsmouth, NH 03801
Telephone: 800-793-2154
Fax: 603-431-7840
http://www.heinemann.com

Heinle and Heinle
25 Thomson Place
Boston, MA 02210
Telephone: 617-289-7700
Fax: 617-289-7855
http://www.heinle.com

Houghton Mifflin
222 Berkeley Street
Boston, MA 02116
Telephone: 800-733-3052
Fax: 800-733-1810
http://www.hmco.com

Intercultural Press
PO Box 700
Yarmouth, ME 04096
Telephone: 800-370-2665
Fax: 207-846-5181
http://www.interculturalpress.com

JAG Publications
11288 Ventura Boulevard, Suite 301
Studio City, CA 91604
Telephone: 818-505-9002
Fax: 818-505-9002
http://www.jagpublications-esl.com

Jamestown Publishers
Glencoe/McGraw Hill of McGraw-
   Hill Education
1221 Avenue of the Americas
New York, NY 10020
http://www.glencoe.com/gln/jamestown

McGraw-Hill Higher Education
Two Penn Plaza, 21st Floor
New York, NY 10121
Telephone: 212-904-6443
Fax: 212-904-4883
http://mhhe.com

National Textbook Company/School
4255 West Touhy Avenue
Lincolnwood, IL 60712
Telephone: 800-621-1918
Fax: 800-998-3103
http://www.ntc-school.com

New Readers Press
1320 Jamesville Avenue
Syracuse, NY 13210
Telephone: 800-448-8878
Fax: 315-422-5561
http://www.newreaderspress.com

Oxford University Press
198 Madison Ave
New York, NY 10016
Telephone: 212-726-6300
Fax: 212-726-6391
http://www.oup-usa.org

Pearson Education
10 Bank Street, Suite 900
White Plains, NY 10606
Telephone: 914-993-5000
Fax: 914-997-8115
http://www.pearsoned-elt.com

Prentice Hall Regents
One Lake Street
Upper Saddle River, NJ 07458
Telephone: 800-375-2375
http://www.phregents.com

Pro Lingua Associates
20 Elm Street
Brattleboro, VT 05301
Telephone: 800-366-4775
Fax: 802-257-5117
800-366-4775
http://www.ProLinguaAssociates.com

Steck-Vaughn
PO Box 26015
Austin, TX 78755
Telephone: 800-531-5015
Fax: 512-343-6854
http://www.steck-vaughn.com

TESOL
700 South Washington Street, Suite 200
Alexandria, VA 22314
Telephone: 703-836-0774
Fax: 703-836-7864
http://www.tesol.org

TOEFL (Educational Testing Service)
Rosedale Road MS 49-L
Princeton, NJ 08541
Telephone: 609-683-2052
Fax: 609-279-9146
http://www.toefl.org

University of Michigan Press
PO Box 1104
839 Greene Street
Ann Arbor, MI 48106
Telephone: 734-764-4392
Fax: 800-876-1922
http://www.press.umich.edu

APPENDIX D:
Organizations of Interest to ESL Tutors

Teachers of English to Speakers of Other Languages, Inc. (TESOL)
700 South Washington Street, Suite 200
Alexandria, VA 22314
Telephone: 703-836-0774
Fax: 703-836-7864
E-mail: info@tesol.org
http://www.tesol.org

TESOL's mission is to develop the expertise of its members and others involved in teaching English to speakers of other languages to help them foster effective communication in diverse settings while respecting individuals' language rights. To this end:

- *TESOL articulates and advances standards for professional preparation and employment, continuing education, and student programs.*
- *TESOL links groups worldwide to enhance communication among language specialists.*
- *TESOL produces high-quality programs, services, and products.*
- *TESOL promotes advocacy to further the profession.*

(About TESOL, http://www.tesol.org)

American Council on the Teaching of Foreign Languages (ACTFL)
6 Executive Plaza
Yonkers, NY 10701
Telephone: 914-963-8830
Fax: 914-963-1275
E-mail: actflhq@aol.com
http://www.actfl.org

> *[ACTFL] is the only national organization dedicated to the improvement and expansion of the teaching and learning of all languages at all levels of instruction. ACTFL is an individual membership organization of more than 7,000 foreign language educators and administrators from elementary through graduate education, as well as government and industry.*
>
> (*About ACTFL*, http://www.actfl.org)

American Library Association (ALA) Resources for Parents, Teens and Kids
50 East Huron
Chicago, IL 60611
Telephone: 800-545-2433
Fax: 312-440-9374
http://www.ala.org/parents

> *The American Library Association provides leadership for the development, promotion, and improvement of library and information services and the profession of librarianship in order to enhance learning and ensure access to information for all.*
>
> (http://www.ala.org; July 12, 2002)

Association for Supervision and Curriculum Development (ASCD)
1703 North Beauregard Street
Alexandria, VA 22311-1714
Telephone: 703-578-9600, 800-933-ASCD
Fax: 703-575-5400
http://www.ascd.org

> *The Association for Supervision and Curriculum Development is a unique international, nonprofit, nonpartisan association of professional educators whose jobs cross all grade levels and subject areas. In their diversity, [its] members share a profound commitment to excellence in education. Founded in 1943, ASCD's mission is to forge covenants in teaching and learning for the success of all learners.*
>
> (*About ASCD*, http://www.ascd.org/aboutascd.html)

Center for Applied Linguistics (CAL)
4646 40th Street NW
Washington, DC 20016-1859
Telephone: 202-362-0700
Fax: 202-362-3740
http://www.cal.org

CAL is a private, non-profit organization: a group of scholars and educators who use the findings of linguistics and related sciences in identifying and addressing language-related problems. CAL carries out a wide range of activities including research, teacher education, analysis and dissemination of information, design and development of instructional materials, technical assistance, conference planning, program evaluation, and policy analysis.

(About CAL, http://www.cal.org/admin/about.html) Also houses the National Clearinghouse for ESL Literacy Education (http://www.cal.org/ncle), a worthwhile resource site funded by the U.S. Department of Education.

International Reading Association (IRA)
800 Barksdale Road
PO Box 8139
Newark, DE 19714-8139
Telephone: 302-731-1600, ext. 224
Fax: 302-737-0878
http://www.reading.org

The International Reading Association is a professional membership organization dedicated to promoting high levels of literacy for all by improving the quality of reading instruction, disseminating research and information about reading, and encouraging the lifetime reading habit. Our members include classroom teachers, reading specialists, consultants, administrators, supervisors, university faculty, researchers, psychologists, librarians, media specialists, and parents.

(About the Association, http://www.reading.org/about/)

Laubach Literacy
1320 Jamesville Avenue
Syracuse, NY 13210
Telephone: 315-422-9121, 888-LAUBACH (528-2224)
http://www.laubach.org

Laubach Literacy is a nonprofit educational corporation dedicated to helping adults of all ages improve their lives and their communities by learning reading, writing, math and problem-solving skills.

Laubach's U.S. Program Division has 1,100 member programs throughout the United States. Our International Programs Division has partner programs teaching people in 1,008 communities in 36 countries in Africa, Asia, the Middle East and Latin America.

Our publishing division, New Readers Press, publishes and distributes 500 titles of books and other educational materials to 30,000 literacy programs, libraries, schools, prisons, and religious organizations nationwide.

(About Laubach Literacy, http://www.laubach.org/ABOUTUS/indexaboutus.html)

Literacy Volunteers of America (LVA)
PO Box 73275
Washington, DC 20056
Telephone: 202-387-1772
Fax: 202-588-0714
http://www.literacyvolunteers.org

> *Literacy Volunteers of America, Inc. (LVA) is a fully integrated national network of local, state, and regional literacy providers that give adults and their families the opportunity to acquire skills to be effective in their roles as members of their families, communities, and workplaces.*
>
> *LVA's cost-effective system enables us to provide student-focused tutoring, one-to-one or in small groups, at no charge to the student.*
>
> *Our mission is to change lives through literacy.*
>
> (http://www.literacyvolunteers.org/home/index.htm)

NAFSA: Association of International Educators
1307 New York Avenue, NW
Eighth Floor
Washington, DC 20005-401
Telephone: 202-737-3699
Fax: 202-737-3657
E-mail: inbox@nafsa.org
http://www.nafsa.org

> *NAFSA: Association of International Educators promotes the exchange of students and scholars to and from the United States. The Association sets and upholds standards of good practice and provides professional education and training that strengthen institutional programs and services related to international educational exchange. NAFSA provides a forum for discussion of issues and a network for sharing information as it seeks to increase awareness of and support for international education in higher education, in government, and in the community.*
>
> *A majority of NAFSA's members can be found on college and university campuses working as foreign student advisers and admissions officers, study abroad advisers, directors of international programs, teachers of English as a second language, administrators of intensive English programs, overseas educational advisers, community volunteers, and administrators of sponsored exchange programs.*
>
> (*About NAFSA*, http://www.nafsa.org/Template.cfm?Section=InsideNafsa &NavMenuID=4)

National Clearinghouse for English Language Acquisition (NCELA)
The George Washington University
Center for the Study of Language & Education
2011 Eye Street NW, Suite 200
Washington, DC 20006
Telephone: 202-467-0867
Fax: 800-531-9347
E-mail: askncbe@ncbe.gwu.edu
http://www.ncbe.gwu.edu

NCELA, the National Clearinghouse for English Language Acquisition and Language Instruction Educational Programs (formerly NCBE, the National Clearinghouse for Bilingual Education) is funded by the U.S. Department of Education's Office of English Language Acquisition, Language Enhancement & Academic Achievement for Limited English Proficient Students (OELA, formerly OBEMLA) to collect, analyze, and disseminate information relating to the effective education of linguistically and culturally diverse learners in the U.S.

NCELA provides information through its web site and topical publications, and produces a weekly electronic news bulletin, Newsline, *and a monthly electronic magazine,* Outlook.

(About the National Clearinghouse, http://www.ncbe.gwu.edu/about.htm*)*

National Council of Teachers of English (NCTE)
1111 West Kenyon Road
Urbana, IL 61801-1096
Telephone: 800-369-6283
Fax: 217-328-9645
E-mail: public_info@ncte.org
http://www.ncte.org

The National Council of Teachers of English is devoted to improving the teaching and learning of English and the language arts at all levels of education. Since 1911, NCTE has provided a forum for the profession, an array of opportunities for teachers to continue their professional growth throughout their careers, and a framework for cooperation to deal with issues that affect the teaching of English.

(About NCTE, http://www.ncte.org/about*)*

United States Department of Education
400 Maryland Avenue SW
Washington, DC 20202-0498
Telephone:1-800-USA-LEARN
E-mail: CustomerService@inet.ed.gov
http://www.ed.gov

The U.S. Department of Education was established on May 4, 1980 by Congress in the Department of Education Organization Act (Public Law 96-88 of October 1979). The Department's mission is to:

- *Strengthen the Federal commitment to assuring access to equal educational opportunity for every individual;*

- *Supplement and complement the efforts of states, the local school systems and other instrumentalities of the states, the private sector, public and private nonprofit educational research institutions, community-based organizations, parents, and students to improve the quality of education;*

- *Encourage the increased involvement of the public, parents, and students in Federal education programs;*

- *Promote improvements in the quality and usefulness of education through Federally supported research, evaluation, and sharing of information;*

- *Improve the coordination of Federal education programs;*

- *Improve the management of Federal education activities; and*

- *Increase the accountability of Federal education programs to the President, the Congress, and the public.*

(About ED—Our Mission, http://www.ed.gov/about/mission.jsp)

The Authors

Teresa S. Dalle is an associate professor of English at the University of Memphis. She has been teaching ESL since 1974 and educating teachers since 1984. She also conducts teacher education courses and workshops, directs practica for ESL student teachers, and researches in the area of application of theory to practice in ESL. She has published numerous papers on various topics related to the teaching of ESL.

Laurel J. Young runs her own tutoring business, Language Access Tutoring Service, in which she works with students of all ages to help them develop English language skills. She contracts with schools and businesses to provide English tutoring to specific groups and also provides help and advice to many individuals on tutoring as a profession. She has presented at regional meetings of ESL teachers.

Index

✦ G

Games
    sources for, 185
    as teaching tool, 2–3, 27, 29, 142
GED. *See* General Educational Development test
General Educational Development test (GED), 188
    preparation for, 118–119, 152
German, English cognates in, 78t
Gestures, teaching about, 138–140
GMAT. *See* Graduate Management Admission Test
Goals
    of lesson plan, setting, 85
    of student, determining, 49, 59f
    of tutoring
        design of, 61–67, 68f
        fulfillment of, evaluating, 63
Goldstein, S., 26
Government agencies, as resource, 30–31
Graduate Management Admission Test (GMAT), 188
    preparation for, 118–119, 152
Graduate Record Examination (GRE), 188
    preparation for, 152
Graham, C., 26, 95
Graham, C. R., 113–115
Grammar
    assessment of, 51
    lesson plan for, 97–98
        format of, 38
        overgeneralization of rules in, 76
        reference books on, 26, 175–177
        teaching of, 64–65
            tips for, 106–107
            to young children, 14–15
Grant, L., 8–10, 26, 178
Graph(s)
    sample of, 144f
    use of, 133–134
Graphic organizers
    definition of, 135
    samples of, 145–147, 185
    uses of, 135–137
    value of, 131
GRE. *See* Graduate Record Examination
Guided questions, 106
Guidelines for Writing Skill Levels, 49

✦ H

Harcourt College Publishers, 192
Hartmann, P., 136–137, 137f
Hearing problems, 19
Heinemann, Inc., 192
Heinle & Heinle, Inc., 192
High/low reading materials, 28, 98
Homework
    assigning, 88
    Internet exercises as, 113
    review of, 86
Houghton Mifflin, Inc., 192
Household items, as teaching tools, 27–28. *See also* Realia
Humor, importance of, 73

✦ I

Idioms, texts on, 177
Information gathering, 13–21, 36. *See also* Assessment
    age, 14–16
    culture, 17–18
    education level, 19
    native language/other languages, 16–17
    needs of student, 15, 18, 43
    personal information, 13
    previous English study, 18
    Student Information Card, 13, 14f, 19, 21f, 36, 167
    Teacher Information Form, 6, 37, 40f, 49
    years of residency in U.S., 18
Information organizer, 147f
Integrated series textbooks, 26–27, 180–181
Interactions series, 26
Intercultural Press, 192
Interference errors, 16–17, 75–76
Interlanguage, 76, 188
Intermediate-level students
    appropriate instruction for, 63
    assessment of reading skills, 55–56
    books for
        dictionaries, 174
        grammars, 175–176
        on idioms, 177
        on listening/speaking, 177–178
        readers, 179
        on writing, 182
    characteristics of, 45, 54t, 57t, 58t

Also Available From TESOL

Action Research
Julian Edge, Editor

Bilingual Education
Donna Christian and Fred Genesee, Editors

Distance-Learning Programs
Lynn E. Henrichsen, Editor

Implementing the ESL Standards for Pre-K–12 Students Through Teacher Education
Marguerite Ann Snow, Editor

Integrating the ESL Standards Into Classroom Practice: Grades Pre-K–2
Betty Ansin Smallwood, Editor

Integrating the ESL Standards Into Classroom Practice: Grades 3–5
Katharine Davies Samway, Editor

Integrating the ESL Standards Into Classroom Practice: Grades 6–8
Suzanne Irujo, Editor

Integrating the ESL Standards Into Classroom Practice: Grades 9–12
Barbara Agor, Editor

Intensive English Programs in Postsecondary Settings
Nicholas Dimmitt and Maria Dantas-Whitney, Editors

Internet for English Teaching
Mark Warschauer, Heidi Shetzer, and Christine Meloni

Journal Writing
Jill Burton and Michael Carroll, Editors

Standards for Adult Education ESL Programs
TESOL

Reading and Writing in More Than One Language: Lessons for Teachers
Elizabeth Franklin, Editor

Teacher Education
Karen E. Johnson, Editor

Teaching in Action: Case Studies From Second Language Classrooms
Jack C. Richards, Editor

Technology-Enhanced Learning Environments
Elizabeth Hanson-Smith, Editor

For more information, contact
Teachers of English to Speakers of Other Languages, Inc.
700 South Washington Street, Suite 200
Alexandria, Virginia 22314 USA
Tel 703-836-0774 • Fax 703-836-6447 • publications@tesol.org • http://www.tesol.org/